The Tagger

and other stories

Edited by Ginger Mayerson

The Wapshott Press

The Tagger and Other Stories

Published by
The Wapshott Press
An Imprint of J LHLS
PO Box 31513
Los Angeles, CA 90031

The Wapshott Press
www.WapshottPress.com

First printing February 2009

"The Tagger" originally appeared in The Velvet Mafia, Issue 16, 2006.

ISBN: 978-0-615-26249-9

06 05 04 03   4 3 2 1

Wapshott Press logo by Molly Kiely

Mark, by Molly Kiely

Contents

Mick by Molly Kiely

The Tagger

Ginger Mayerson

The thump on the sidewalk outside his studio sounded larger than a cat jumping or a rat falling out of a tree. There were, in fact, no trees outside Paul's studio. There was, however, a billboard, which was a magnet for taggers. Another case for it being a human thump were the police sirens and the running feet. Against his better judgment, he looked outside.

"Not you again," he said to the kid, who was struggling to stand. Well, at this distance, Paul realized he was more of a late teenager or in his early twenties than a kid.

"Who me?" he said, wincing in pain and favoring his left leg.

"Yes, you. You who fell off this same billboard last weekend, you."

The sirens were getting closer. The kid limped behind Paul's van parked next to the studio. There was a plea for help in his eyes as he melted into the shadows.

A patrol car slowed to a halt in front of Paul. The cop stuck his head out and asked if he'd seen anyone tagging the billboard. Paul said he hadn't seen anyone on the billboard, which was true. This satisfied the cop and, after wishing Paul a pleasant evening, he drove off.

After years of living in an industrial area much beloved by taggers and junkies, Paul knew that taggers, at least, were not dangerous unless they were cornered. He'd never had occasion or desire to corner one, so there'd never been any conflicts with them. Paul minded his own business, only nodding when the spray can-toting outlaws made eye-contact, which was seldom. Now, the kid tonight he'd seen before: he'd been trying to tag the new billboards above his studio for several weeks. That particular billboard changed frequently enough that it was a challenge to keep it tagged. It seemed to be the personal quest of this one particular kid to keep it tagged and he was willing to brave cold, rain, police, and falls. Paul had seen him fall more than once, but the kid usually bounced right up again and darted away before the police got there. But not that night.

"Hey, thanks, man," the kid said, hobbling out of the shadows.

"You're not going to get far on that leg," Paul said. "And the cops are probably just going around the block, looking for someone who has spray paint on his pants. Like you do."

"I–" the kid slipped back in the shadows as a car went by. "I'll be okay," he said, trying to look tough balanced on one leg.

"I can give you a ride somewhere," Paul said.

The kid thought about it and then agreed. He directed Paul into a shabby neighborhood not far from the train station. He said, "Thanks," and hobbled away as Paul drove off.

"You're welcome. Stay off that billboard, kid," Paul thought ruefully as he drove home. He stopped at the market to pick up a carton of milk because he knew Mark would be there when he got home and he knew he wouldn't feel like explaining where he'd been.

"Where've you been?" Mark asked after a quick kiss hello.

"I went to get milk. I was out," Paul said, putting the carton in his nearly empty fridge.

"Thanks." Mark could not drink his morning coffee without milk. It was very nice of Paul to remember this even though Paul had become distant since Mark moved out. This small consideration seemed like an encouraging sign.

A week later, Paul noticed the billboard was half

tagged. He'd been at Mark's place the night before, so the kid must have been back and gotten interrupted again. "Idiot," he murmured as he let himself into his studio. The kid was an idiot with a quest, and the romantic in Paul couldn't help but admire that.

Making Mark fall in love with him had once been a quest, but an accomplished quest is no longer as interesting as an unaccomplished one. Reasonable as ever, Mark had suggested they needed more space or something and moved out. They continued to date, but Paul was keeping his options open. In these last, restless months before his thirtieth birthday, Paul was no longer sure what his options were open for, but they were definitely open.

A few days after this, the half-tagged billboard was changed. Paul had nearly forgotten about the tagger, when late one evening there was a slightly panicky knock on the door and then a louder banging.

"Police officers, open up."

Paul looked through the peephole and there were indeed two cops standing behind the kid Paul now thought of as his tagger. He opened the door.

"Do you know this kid?" one of the cops asked.

"Sure," Paul said, hoping they would not ask his name. "I even know where he lives," he added before they could ask. "Miss your bus again, pal?" he asked the tagger as if he'd known him all his life. "Need a ride home?"

"Yeah, sorry, thanks," the kid mumbled.

The cops looked on dubiously and seemed about to ask some hard questions, but whatever they heard on their patrol car radio caused them to leave in a hurry. Paul hustled the kid inside before they could change their minds and come back.

"Whew, thanks, mister," the tagger said.

"My name's Paul. What's yours?"

"Daniel."

"You should give up the tagger life, Daniel," Paul said, watching the kid stroll around his studio. "Before you end up in jail."

"Someday," Daniel said vaguely. "What do ya do here?" he asked, inspecting Paul's G5s.

"Computer games." Paul made a quick mental review of the window bar situation, his homeowners policy, and the wisdom of letting this strange, reckless kid into his studio.

"Cool. Wanna go to an art opening?"

"At this hour?" Paul looked at his watch.

"Sure, if we go now, we'll beat the rush at midnight."

The art show was in a tiny, dark club under a freeway. It was too dark to see any art, so Paul figured it was just an excuse for a bunch of tough guys to stand really close to each other. The music was too loud to talk over, but everyone was swaying a little to it, not that it could be called dancing, but it was more than just standing. There were male couples and threesomes standing in dark corners, doing more than swaying. It looked to Paul as if they were jacking each other off.

"What kind of place have you brought me to, Daniel?" Paul wondered, swaying close to him, inhaling the thick clouds of dope smoke and male pheromones.

Eventually Daniel maneuvered them into a dark alcove and fumbled at Paul's belt. With a little more fumbling, they were jacking each other off in rhythm to the music. "I don't kiss," Daniel growled when Paul leaned toward him.

Paul thought that was a shame; he liked to kiss and Daniel had a nice mouth. The nearly forgotten Mark liked to kiss and was good at it. At least he was good at kissing Paul. But Paul was too busy coming, and feeling Daniel climax was too distracting, to pursue this train of thought any further.

They zipped up, drank some beer, and when the place seemed even more crowded, they left. Paul dropped him in the same shabby neighborhood as before and went home to wash the smell of sweat, semen, and dope off his body.

Thereafter, Paul kept an eye on the billboard to see

if it was tagged. He was also half listening for the sound of a body falling off it. Neither of those things happened. He was distracted and when Mark, who was considering moving back in, asked him what was up, he said, "Work," as if that explained everything. Mark didn't pry, but he stopped talking about moving back in.

A few weeks later there was a soft tap on his door late one night. "I was wondering what became of you," Paul said. He stepped aside to let Daniel in, but the kid stayed put.

"Hey, c'mon, I wanna show you something," Daniel said. "Bring your car, okay?"

In the car, Daniel alternated between giving directions and molesting Paul's thigh. "You like guys, right?"

"Yeah, you?" Paul asked.

"Yeah, but I keep it on the down-low."

"What's that?" Paul asked. He parked the car near the concrete ravine train tracks ran through.

"I like to come, and girls are too much work sometimes. Another guy, he understand that, too." Daniel got out of the car and sat on the hood.

Paul followed him, thinking that even though Mark was a lot of work, at least he liked to kiss as well as come.

"So we keep it on the down-low and everyone's happy," Daniel said, running his hand over the bulge in Paul's jeans.

"Is that why we're here?" Paul asked, sliding his hand around Daniel's waist.

"Nah, we're waiting for the moon," Daniel said. He pulled Paul against him, pushed the older guy's legs apart and leaned their crotches together. His mouth was inches from Paul's, but Paul controlled himself and concentrated on getting his and Daniel's cocks out.

Daniel leaned his forehead against Paul's collarbone and ran his hand down their dicks, pressing them together in a voluptuous, maddening rhythm. Sliding together their cocks slick with pre-come, the tagger varied the tempo and pressure, spinning the tease out until Paul thought he'd lose his fucking mind. He came first, with a gasp, his cock jerking against Daniel's. And then Daniel let loose with a grunt that ended in a whimper. The night was very quiet as they held each against the hood of Paul's car.

"Thanks," Paul said, and wiped his hands on his jeans.

"Welcome," Daniel said, and wiped his hands on Paul's jeans. "There's the moon. Look." He pointed at the ravine wall opposite their perch.

There was a huge tag, maybe several smaller ones and some designs Paul had seen on buildings in the area, but had never seen so deliberately arranged before. "Yours?" he asked.

"Me and some guys," Daniel said, proudly. "I did the stuff mostly on the left."

"That's the best part," Paul said, and got a killer smile as thanks. They stared at it until clouds covered the moon up.

Back in the car, Daniel said, "I'm leaving in a few days. I'm joining the Marines."

"No more down-low there, pal," Paul thought, but said, "Congratulations. They don't just take anyone."

"Yeah, they got the best deal, too," Daniel said. "I might go to art school when I get out."

"You could do that now," Paul thought, but said, "Ah, good idea, you could be an artist."

He dropped him in the same shabby neighborhood and drove home. Paul never saw him again, but a few days later the billboard was tagged and the word "bye" was spray painted on his front door.

The next day Paul asked Mark to move back in and give it another try. After one last fling, even on the down-low, with a reckless, romantic kid like Daniel, he could settle down with Mark, not on the down low, and have no regrets or what-might-have-beens whatsoever.

The End

Across the Universe

Laura Dearlove

It had been a normal Saturday before that. He went for a walk; the heat came off the pavements, bounced between the buildings, boxed-in and stifling. He wasn't really heading anywhere in particular, down the high street, maybe toward the common, maybe it would be cooler on the grass or maybe it would just be crammed in with sunbathers and dogs and pushchairs and runners...

He was wearing yesterday's t-shirt and he hadn't done anything with his hair when he'd rolled out of bed. That was what he would remember, afterwards, that was what he would think of. If he'd known. Worn a fresh t-shirt, washed his hair, locked all his doors and windows, handcuffed himself to his bed, surely something would have worked, even for just a day, just given him one more day...

Because "perfectly normal" was about to end, for him, forever.

A hand catching his wrist. "Chris Stephenson. Right?"

He turned. Grey-eyed, blond-haired, cockily-smiling man with scattered freckles and a great deal of knowing amusement in his eyes. "Yes?" he said. "You're..."

He ran through parties he'd been to, people he'd met at work, could not place the face. Could not, for the life of him, place that evil grinning face.

"Jack Smith. Love of your life. Let me buy you a coffee."

***

It's hard to say no to someone dragging you by the wrist. Someone who knows your name and pulls you along and talks, pretty much continuously, about things you're not entirely sure make sense.

"Look at this weather! Last time it was raining like, shit, the end of the world or something, not that you looked bad in that wet shirt, you were a much smarter dresser last time. Not that I mind the casual look at all, bet those jeans look damn good just riding on your hips. So what do you do this time? Something important in a magazine last time around, hence the shirt, and we fucked against the window in your office thirty floors up or something. A*maz*ing views. I like you in a tie. Like you out of a tie, of course, I just *like* you. You'll be a white Americano, right? Half a sachet of sugar. That is weird, by the way, I always tell you that. Half a sachet. Like, pour it in or don't, you know? Halfway is just–"

"Excuse me," Chris said, trying to pry his wrist free, "but who the hell are–"

He lost the end of the sentence and his breath being dumped into a chair outside a coffee shop, and the blond madman said, "Be right back, keep the table warm!" and strolled inside. And Chris sat, too stunned to move, even though the sight of the open pavement and possibility of running looked so damn good right then.

But he knew how he took his coffee. That was weird, knowing that. And he knew his name, and -

Jack Smith. Love of your life.
We fucked against the window in your office.
I just like *you.*

...had he wandered out of a care in the community center or something? Maybe Chris *did* need to get out of here, maybe–

He stood up, and Jack's hand on his shoulder batted him down.

"Chill! Coffee's here. Iced coffee, might as well make the most of the weather. So, c'mon, what's the story this time around? How are you, first of all? You look well," said a little more quietly, a little less breezily, and his eyes tracked Chris's face like he was looking over an old friend for the last time. Chris just stared at him.

"I'm sorry, honestly I'm sorry, obviously we must have met before but...who are you?"

Jack sat back, and rubbed his forehead, and grinned.

"I get tired of going through this every time, you know that? Jack Smith, I told you that. Jack Arnold Smith. Don't tell anyone about the Arnold. I'm the love of your life, but we've only got the twenty-four hours so try not to ask too many dumb questions, all right? I'll be gone again by the morning."

"Gone...what?"

"The next universe," he said, and shrugged, and took a mouthful of coffee. "Traveling on. It's nothing personal. It's never personal, I'd always spend the rest of my life with you. But that's just how it works."

He'd been offered one wish. "Just the one. Not three?" he'd asked, and batted his eyelashes. But no, just one. Threes are for fairy tales.

So he weighed up his options and decided that the songs on the radio were right, and he made his choice. True love, he said. Whatever else you could get by with that, right? True love.

True love is complicated, he'd been told. He'd just shrugged. Sure, that's fine, he'd take the complications. It'd be worth it, right?

It had its moments, totally. Seeing him again for the first time every time, getting that puzzled crease above his nose, seeing the way his eyebrows folded as he tried to recognize him. Seeing him in every city, in every life. Always a first kiss. Always a first touch, a first word, a first time. Because the love of his life–was complicated. It was *him*.

But it could have been any of him...

"Twenty four hours in each universe," he said. "I'm beginning to run out of count of universes, like, shit, this better not be infinite, you know? A guy needs a rest, even from you." And then, "No, that's not true. Not from you. I can keep doing it, if there's always you."

"Keep doing...what, exactly? None of this–"

"Look, dude, I have done this plenty of times, okay? So trust me on this. You will complain and huff and tell me I don't make any sense. You will pout your pretty pout and scowl your sexy scowl and then my charms will work their way through and we will have a few brief hours of bliss and then that, for us, will be it. So if we could cut down on the pouting and the scowling, as much as I do like them, we get more of the bliss, okay? Simple mathematics."

Chris stared at him over his coffee and said, "You are insane."

Jack gazed lazily back and said, "I am in love. It is very much the same thing."

And he went off into a ramble about the Greeks and how they understood that true love was madness, erotic insanity, obsession to the point where your brain melts out your ears and your better judgment means nothing and all you are is love for the beloved, wild and aching and crazy and screaming. "And they totally got the whole pretty boy thing too, they really understood the appeal, none of the fucked-up hangups people are dealing with these days, just a lot of happy shagging, which we could be doing right now, you realize that? I have never yet met a you who wanted to go straight to the happy shagging. An infinite universe of you and you never go right to the happy shagging. Dude. *Issues*."

Chris's face was as red as something burnt. "Why do you keep talking about us having sex?"

"Because it's happened." Jack played with his mug a bit, twisting his wrists, tilting it back and forth. "I mean, not *you* and me but me and you, it's happened. And it will happen again, over and over again, you and me. We're forever, but only ever for twenty-four hours. Or like, eighteen hours or something now. We are losing time like the ozone layer is losing integrity or whatever the hell is happening up there. You want to get ice cream or something? We've never got ice cream before. That would be cool, I'd like to do that."

"Ice..."

"Where are we, anyway?"

"You don't even–? Clapham. We're on Clapham–"

"We're in *London*? There's a London in this universe and we are in it. So it's decided, that's perfect, come on." He was already standing up. "Ice cream. I know the place. Get the chocolate, seriously, god it's perfect, it's a slab of perfection in a cone–"

Chris stared up at him. "I don't even know who the hell you *are*."

"You never do, that's how it works, but you will. And anyway, I know you. I know everything about you."

"Like what?" he asked, and folded his arms.

He was so *difficult*. Why did Jack's one true love have to be such a stubborn prat on every world? Beautiful dark eyes scowling (sexy, sexy scowl) and dark hair skimming his eyebrows, mad hair, he'd worn it much shorter in the last universe, and looking at the frown on his gorgeous lips Jack just...fell in love all over again. This man, god, this man, he was doomed to love this man forever and he was so, so, so, so, *so* fucking *lucky*.

"You always take half a sachet of sugar in your coffee. When you read you hunch yourself up like you're trying to climb into the book. You like big books, you always have tons of sci-fi, and if you haven't read him yet you will *love* Dostoyevsky. You have a birthmark shaped almost exactly like India just beside your groin. You love the Beatles. You always do, in every universe, you always love the Beatles, you're such a dinosaur. You are never indifferent to bananas. In some universes you hate them and in some you love them but you're never indifferent. You put the milk in the bowl before your cereal because you're a freak.

When you were a kid you had a stuffed monkey called–"

"How the *hell*–"

"You're the love of my life. We're meant to be together."

"You're insane."

"We only have today."

"You are completely raving. How do you know all this? Are you stalking me?"

"Come get ice cream with me."

"You are..."

"C'mon. It's such a nice day."

Chris stared up at him and Jack wished they'd already worked through this, wished he could just pull him up into his arms right now and kiss him with his hands slipped into the back pockets of his jeans, kiss him and close his eyes and really, really feel him.

Chris had lost his mind.

He was walking along the south bank of the Thames, underneath the tourist-dripping hulk of Tower bridge, eating ice cream with a madman who knew his name and how he took his coffee and apparently *everything else about him*. Everything. Down to the kind of underwear he preferred and how much he loved clean sheets on the bed. Everything.

And he thought Chris was amazing. And gorgeous, as he kept telling him. Sexy and intelligent and funny and just fucking wonderful. "Of course it's you. In every world you. I can't believe how right they got that, the true love thing, always you and you are just– god, like, the most incredible person on the planet. But every time it's not like you're just this great homogenous mass of *yous*, you know? It's always...you." And his hungry grey eyes read over Chris's face like he might never see him again. "Because you are just...I'm not gonna make it 'round this infinite set of universes, you know that? My heart's gonna pack out before too long. You just make me–"

"Do you ever stop talking?"

"I do when you kiss me. Which you haven't done yet."

"I'm...eating ice cream."

"Oh, excuses."

"How do you even know I'm gay?"

"Sexuality is irrelevant. It's about us."

"How can you fall in love with someone you never meet for more than a day?"

"Because it's you."

Chris glanced at him, saw how perfectly serious his eyes were, and scowled off to the side, across the river. Summer sunlight blinked bright Morse code off the windows of the buildings in the City, and gleamed and chopped over the surface of the water. There was just enough breeze to make the day pleasant, and the ice cream was, yes, very good, bought from an Italian stall almost underneath the bridge. And...

He cut a sly glance back across at Jack, who was licking almost down to his hand to catch a drip before it hit skin. And Jack looked up at him, and smiled, and something deep inside Chris's chest went *boom boom boom boom.*

"Why should I even believe you? Jumping across universes..."

"To you. Always to you."

"How do you always find me?"

"I'm always placed near you. I don't know, I just always do. What do you do in this world, by the way? Did we actually get that far?"

"I...I work in a botanical center, actually, I work with rare breeds of...Why are you smiling?"

"I'm imagining you in a white vest. All smeared with dirt. Pushing a wheelbarrow, just a gleam of sweat across the brow, you stop to wipe it with your wrist–"

"Shut up, it's not like that, it's–"

"You'd be good with plants. You're very gentle, very patient. I can imagine you with your hands in the soil." His eyes watchful, serious grey, like the waters of the Thames. "I think you're probably happier than he was, in his big shiny office thirty floors up."

Chris just stared at him for a moment. "Do you miss the ones you leave behind?"

Jack looked at his ice cream, licked it, swallowed. Then he said, "I already know what it's like to go to sleep with you in my arms. But I have never in my life woken up with you at my side."

Chris looked down into his own ice cream, felt the blush hard in his skin and he didn't know why, blinked hard a couple of times and Jack murmured, "Don't."

He rubbed at Chris's wrist, squeezed it. "Hey. Don't. Don't, honestly, I get upset enough for the both of us–"

"I'm sorry–"

"It's all right. Really, it's all right. It's just how it is, it's what happens when you don't read the small print on your wish. And how is it bad?"

Jack's fingers were warm on Chris's skin, his thumb pressing and stroking at the wrist bone, his fingers settled and protective around the wrist. "If it wasn't like this I'd never have met you, would I?"

Chris stared at Jack's hand on his wrist, holding it so easily as if he'd held it a thousand times before.

"You're too skinny on every world," Jack said, and smiled softly.

Chris pulled his wrist free, just gently, and began trying to deal with the sticky rivers of ice cream on his other hand. Jack sighed, and looked out across the river, and said, "You have a heart the size of a whale or something. I don't know anymore if I love you for that or just love it because it's a part of you."

"Why me?"

"Because you're perfect."

"Why always *me*–?"

"Because you're always perfect." He smiled at him and Chris pretended he was too busy mopping up ice cream to see. "Chris, Chris. I love you."

***

At least they spoke the same language on this world, that could always be a barrier. They still found each other, even if they didn't share a single word they still worked through it, though it definitely made things more difficult, more interesting. On every world they were just meant to be.

Really he didn't think that he was the one who got the shoddy end of the stick in this deal. He may never wake up with the man he loved at his side, but he always knew he was waking up to him again, all the same, him anew, a new him, always him. But what about the Chrises he left behind, the Chrises he found and convinced, *I love you I love you I love you*, and they woke up and he was gone and what were they ever left with...?

He'd met him as an earnest politician's assistant, more anxious than normal and–this had surprised him– still a virgin, and they'd made love tenderly and carefully and sweetly shy in his little flat with the curtains closed and all the lights off.

He'd met him as a Ph.D. student far too busy, *far* too busy for Jack's insanity, but he hadn't been able to shake him and they'd got talking–and talking–and talking some more until they just fell asleep together in the living room of his student flat, bottles of beer discarded all around them.

He'd met him on the street in a mangy sleeping bag outside a station and he'd said, "Hi, how about I buy you breakfast?" And found him a shelter and talked to him and felt so hopeless he was almost shaking with terror because how could he leave him, the man he loved, to this? So he talked to him, pleaded with him, "You're amazing, can't you see how wonderful you are, you're so, so special, please look after yourself, please take care of yourself, because from tomorrow I can't–"

He'd kissed him, that time. That was all.

He'd met him as a bookseller hemmed in by dust and books and dusty books and he'd seduced him with a shared love of T S Eliot and one of the raunchier John

Donnes. Who knew that *that* Chris would be the kinkiest of the lot? They had sex–all day–in the back room on a desk chair and on the desk and on a box of books and on the floor. He desperately hadn't wanted to let him go, clinging hard to him as if he didn't do it every time, "No, no, let me keep this one, please, just let me keep him, this time, please–"

He loved him. Always he loved him and always he left him and he had no idea how long this would go on. Could there really be infinite universes, always another world, *always*? He would die before he got halfway...

Sometimes he thought he couldn't do it. Always another world, never one love for more than one day. His heart really would give out, just stop beating, just break before it faced it all again. But then–

But then he looked across at Chris looking at him like he was new and fascinating and strange and sort of lovely, and all he felt was want.

Chris took in a long breath of Thames-scented air– seaweed, water, pollution, summer-city heat–and leaned back on the railings over the river, arms folded. "All right. Say for one second, one hypothetical second, one insane, 'my judgment is sleeping or possibly you drugged me' second, that I believe you."

"I never lie to you. Even to get you into bed."

Chris scowled, Jack grinned. Chris tried to ignore how that grin made his stomach clench and spin and swoosh; in the space of just a few hours Jack had turned his internal organs into the chew toy of some huge invisible puppy, and Chris was falling, badly, and knew it...

"*Say* I believe you. Where do you see this going, then? If we have this grand one day together. What do you want us to do with it?"

"I was kind of thinking sex," Jack said, and scratched the side of his nose. "Sex or the London Aquarium, I like the London Aquarium. Hey, with a little imagination we could combine the two–"

"How do I know you're not some pervert stalker and I should be running?"

"Do you feel like I am?"

Chris stared into his eyes, as grey as the Thames, looking so deeply, so determinedly into his. The huge invisible puppy gave his stomach one great *squeeze*.

Jack said, very quietly, "I am *never* going to get to see you again after today. Please don't push me away. This is all we'll ever have."

Chris pressed his lips together tight and held his head high. "You will see me again. Again and again, if your story's true–"

"No. No. They'll never be you. They'll never be *you*, will they?"

Icily, "Do you say that to all of them?"

"You can't get jealous about something you're pretending you don't want! Even if I did, do you think it wouldn't make it true for us? For god's *sake* how can you always be so bloody stubborn? This is all we have so we have to make it enough! I want you! I love you! I always fucking do! And I can't ever see you after tonight, I'll never see you again and why do you think playing these stupid fucking games is as important as the time we're losing every goddamned second I'm not kissing you?"

"...Jack..."

His hand, which had been raising as if he was forcing it not to touch Chris, hesitated. And his look of despair and rage gave way to something mystified, and then heart-breakingly delighted.

He said, "That's the first time you've ever said my name."

Chris paused, his mouth open but silent, and Jack reached out the last little distance and took his wrist. His thumb and fingers rubbed his skin gently, a silent question, and Chris closed his eyes, and there were fireflies underneath his skin where Jack touched it, he could feel the fizz and glow of their lights wending through and around his veins, his bones.

"You can say no. If you want, I mean, you can, I'm not so much bigger'n you, if you give me one good shove I'm gone. You could shove me in the Thames, you've never done that before, if you really want to be unique that'd–"

Chris gritted out without opening his eyes, "Do you ever shut up?"

"I already told you there's only one way to make me do that," Jack said, and kissed him.

Like...

Stars falling through his mouth and dropping, fizzing, into his stomach, like his mouth is pressed to the sun and is burning up in the best way possible, like his lips and tongue run with energy like blue-crawling electricity, like body to body they are separate and one at the same time.

God, Jack knows how to kiss.

God, Jack knows how to kiss *him*.

He hadn't even tidied the flat, and when he held the door open for Jack he felt the embarrassment of the newspapers on the kitchen table and Saturday night's half-folded pizza box sticking out of the recycling bin.

But Jack slid his arms around his waist from behind and whispered, "You have a Doctor Who figure on your telly, you adorable dork, I love you." And kissed him underneath his jaw, Chris with his head tilted back, throat bared and helpless. With a struggle, he didn't whimper.

Trying to walk without peeling themselves apart to the sofa, tripping over discarded trainers and almost slipping on a splayed-open magazine, ("You get New Scientist. Of *course* you get New Scientist. Beautiful, beautiful dork.") thumping side by side onto the sofa cushions and Chris trying not to laugh, now, and he couldn't remember ever feeling this insane, this open, this overwhelmed, this–

"God, you're gorgeous," Jack whispered, still

kissing up his jaw, the skin all turned to nerve endings, his mouth sliding up so he could gently bite his earlobe." We've already wasted so much time." His nose tip brushed Chris's burning earlobe as he began kissing and breathing his way down the side of his neck again, two fingers slipping out the neck of his t-shirt. "If you didn't wanna talk about it so damn much we could've been doing this like five hours ago–"

"I'm the one who talks too much, *I'm* the one who–?"

"Hush hush hush," Jack said happily, and his hand slid inwards over the pocket of Chris's jeans and settled between his legs. The blood immediately shot to Chris's face, and elsewhere entirely.

"Jack–"

"It's all right."

"I-I mean–"

"It's all right, it's me. It's me. Have you done this before?"

"Of course I–"

"Then it's all right, isn't it?" But he stopped kissing his neck, and raised his face, and met Chris's twisted-back eye. "Except this will be different, because this is us."

Chris stared into his eyes and whispered, "I think I've gone insane."

"Nowadays they call it 'falling in love'," Jack said. And smiled his dazzling smile, and when he kissed him Chris was lost.

Through the window into his bedroom, streaks of afternoon sunlight and no use for the sheets in this heat. Jack's hands were sure and firm and knowing and Chris's entire body was reacting to him now anyway, his hand wrapped around his elbow would have been enough to make him come but he was sure that what Jack's other hand was doing at that moment was helping that along. His hands on Chris's thighs and they trembled. His mouth on Chris's belly and it burned. And the whole of him, the beautiful burning aching whole of him, and he felt like he could fall backwards through the bed, felt like he could bend himself the right way and suddenly they'd share a body, felt like their bodies had been designed to move and fit so well, felt like his body and Jack's were on the same frequency and moving together the pitch they hit was going to crack the day in two.

Jack's muffled bellow of his orgasm into the side of his neck, his shuddery panting, and then his kisses, his hands, and Chris called out again and again but didn't realize that until they had stopped.

The sunlight turned heavy with evening but they didn't even close the curtains. They lay side by side on the bed and held hands and Jack made Chris laugh about once every thirty seconds, and made him want to hit him with the pillow about as much. Jack put the radio on, made their hands dance together on the mattress and then the music turned to an R&B bump-and-grind and he tried to get their hands to join in, and even as they laughed that turned into more grinding, more sex, and Chris laying blissful underneath Jack's weight, pressed into the mattress and so hot his skin felt like it might peel off and he didn't care.

They took a shower. That turned into more sex.

They made dinner. That turned into a lot of kissing but sheer hunger held the sex off for a while.

They started watching TV. Somehow that led to more sex.

Trailing his fingers over Jack's shoulder blades, running a hand up to curl in his hair, Chris murmured, "Where are you really from?"

Jack said, muffled into his shoulder, "Another universe."

"Jack, for god's sake, after all this you're still going to keep saying that?"

"Well, I don't like lying to you. And I would say that, you know, for this relationship to work I need you to trust me and believe in me and all but...we really don't need to plan for the long-term, you and me. Believe me on that," he said gloomily. "I don't know why you can't just let this be perfect. It's all we'll ever have."

"But–but you can't be serious–"

"I'm sorry." His arms tightened around Chris's back. "Oh Christ, I really, *really* wish it could be any different from this but– I'm telling the truth, Chris, this is all we have, this day, and I don't want to spend the handful of hours we have left talking about how little time we've got left, okay? Because this has been...this has been incredible. Don't you think? We had coffee, we took a walk, got ice cream, came home, we spent the entire afternoon together, we had some pretty fucking amazing sex if I really do say so myself, we made dinner, watched TV–"

"You can't really call what we were doing in front of the TV watching it."

"–and it was really fucking *nice*, actually. Like a normal day. Like a normal couple. Like maybe next Sunday we'd do the same thing again, and we've done it for months and years already. It was a really, really good day. And I would give my fucking leg, my fucking kidneys, to know I had the rest of my life with you and all the lazy Sundays we could ever want–"

"Jack..."

"But this is all we have and can we just *have* it, please, instead of arguing and whining–"

Chris stroked his hair. "I'm not the one doing the whining."

"Shut up." Jack huffed into his skin.

"That was very definitely a whine."

"Chris, shut up."

"Jack..."

Jack turned his cheek to Chris's shoulder, and stroked his side. "You don't have to say it, really. I know."

Chris closed his eyes, bent his head down and nuzzled into Jack's hair.

Back in bed, everything blue in the not-light night cast through the window, and Jack watched with amused eyes as Chris turned his hand in his, playing his fingers like piano keys, stroking down his thumb, threading their fingers together.

"Do you play the piano?"

"Not for years. Not well, anyway." His eyes glinted up to Jack's, in the night bright and almost black. "Isn't that the sort of thing you should know about me?"

"Not everything in you is universal." He touched Chris's face, felt his cheek, his skin underneath his fingertips. "It's how I always end up falling for you like I've never done it before."

Chris gave him one of his steady, intelligent glares, and Jack tried to ignore it, focused instead on his hair picked out like shards of cut jet against the pillow. "Do I often resent you for having me again and again when I only ever get you for a day?"

"It's not *you*, again and again." Jack said, and ran the backs of his knuckles softly along his cheek. "And you never really believe that I'll be gone in the morning anyway."

He saw the brightness too bright in Chris's eyes in that second, and something stopped his throat as Chris whispered, "Will you really disappear if I go to sleep?"

He made himself smile, but it came out more crooked than he meant. "You can always dream about me."

"What if I don't go to sleep? What if I stay up all night? Never take my eyes off you, never look away–?"

"Don't be crazy. The crazy talk doesn't help, it just makes me slightly afraid."

"I don't want you to go."

"I know."

"I *love* you."

"Oh Jesus," Jack folded him into his arms, breathed him in, pressed him even closer. "Chris, Chris, shit, I love you too..."

On Monday morning his alarm went off and he snapped it off and sat in bed sore and stiff and for half a second, for half a blissful ignorant second, he didn't have any idea why.

Realization was ice water over the head and pooling in the stomach, and he would never be so blessedly ignorant again.

He was alone in the bed; someone had picked one of the discarded sheets up and tucked him under it, because he hadn't gone to sleep underneath one, not in this heat, not up against Jack's warm body, they hadn't needed one...had they? Had he dreamed it?

But the stiffness of his muscles said quite firmly what had happened. And the scent on his sheets remained. And on a basically undeniable level, the stains on the mattress told their own story. Jack had been here. Jack was real. And now Jack had gone.

He sat with his feet flat on the bed, hands in his hair, and put his face down into his knees, trying not to howl.

For a time, he was just dazed. He was sure that around every corner and on every bus he'd bump into Jack. It had been a joke, of course it had been a joke, and he wouldn't care how stupid he'd been made to look if it would just bring him back–

An entire world of communication, mobile phones and emails and letters and newspaper advertisements and he could never get one word through to Jack again. Where was he? Was he really off on another world, with another him? His stomach snarled and squeezed, he looked into the mirror and wanted to punch his own face. Who are you with, where are you? Where *are* you?

His friends didn't know why he didn't want to come out, didn't want to talk on the phone, didn't want to leave his flat. His work colleagues found him even more quiet and self-contained than usual; they left him alone. His mother told him he should buck up, take a holiday. He sat in the flat and listened to the Beatles and waited for Jack to knock at the door.

Jack had ruined *I Will* for him.

Jack had ruined all his favorite music for him. And

he was right, he picked up *Crime and Punishment* when making his zombie way through Borders and he loved Dostoyevsky. He bought every book and read them and ached and felt sick and hated himself and hated Jack as much as he loved him.

He now hated *Across the Universe*.

He hated Jack. He hated Jack and he loved Jack and when he watched Doctor Who he wanted to put a brick through the screen.

Where did you *go*?

Another universe. Another world. Another him. He hated every other him that could possibly exist. He hoped they all died in horrible accidents before Jack could ever get to them so the only Chris there ever was for him to come to was *him*.

After a few weeks it was intolerable. He sat and rotted slowly into his sofa listening to the same old songs and he wanted to die, so he took the easiest decision, the route of least possible thought: buy new music. It was a bright, hot Sunday, the end of the summer, the promise of a mellower autumn in the air and in the sniff of rain not yet in sight. He took a bus out of Clapham, into the city center, and all the people and all the traffic and he felt like an island alone. He walked through the crowds and buggies jammed into from behind, tourists elbowed him aside at the crossings. He couldn't care about anything that wasn't Jack.

He ducked into a music store, high ceilings and not enough air conditioning, and the racks and racks of CDs left him feeling small and hopeless. How to pick out just a handful from this multicolored universe of plastic cases when his head was only full of Jack?

...and behind the counter, talking to another girl at the till with two lip piercings, was a grey-eyed blond-haired man with scattered freckles and a cocky tilt to his mouth as he chattered on like the amused looking girl had nothing else to do with her day than listen to him, like he had all the time in the world...

His heart stopped. When it started again it was so quiet, so sure, so hopeful, so knowing. Jack visited every world where there was a Chris. But why should that mean that those worlds wouldn't contain their own Jacks?

Chris walked over because there was nothing else he could do. The thumping music on the speakers seemed silenced, the shoppers faded away like ghosts, the racks of CDs seemed to part for him. He walked over, and the girl cocked a glance to him, and the blond-haired man chattered on. And he stood at the counter, and the blond-haired man looked at him and did some sort of double take even though his eyes hadn't left Chris' face, no recognition but something else entirely. And Chris said, "Jack Smith? Jack Arnold Smith?"

His mouth fell open. The girl at the till grinned wide and evil and said, "Arnold?"

Chris felt the grin creep up from the inside, forcing his cheeks to bend, and put his hands into his pockets.

"Chris Stephenson. Love of your life. You busy tonight?"

The End

Atlantis

Kitty Johnson

College was Laocoön.

Eddie could never escape. It had been fifteen years since he and Bill had been in the same dorm and dined in the same cafeteria and smoked similar dope and listened to the very same Pink Floyd. Now in 1987 (foreboding number: sounded like a countdown) Eddie was playing the part of a groomsman at Bill's preposterous wedding. The passage of those fifteen years had not earned him a pass from this duty. Eddie was having to, well, not *act* enthused but certainly *emit* a silently enthused vibe over this wedding over which he was actually deeply neutral.

But it was in New Orleans, so that was pretty interesting. Plus the bride's parents were interesting as hell. Rich. At the rehearsal dinner at a restaurant on Bourbon Street (which was so expensive *the waiters picked out the menu for you)* the sky was the frightening limit of how much champagne and beef a man could have.

The rehearsal dinner had been on Friday (which wasn't the whole story of Friday), but now it was Saturday afternoon and the wedding–performed as if a ritual union of sun and moon–was over at last.

On the outside, the rich parents' villa was unassuming with its simple green blinds and white bricks, but the inside was an unthinkable paradise, from the oil portrait of the bride's great-great-grandfather depicted in his Napoleonic general drag ("today he'd be a Shriner" the witty bride had drawled–she was a lawyer) to her mother's Queen of Rex crown hung on a nail from the bathroom door, each careful item spoke of an almost symbolic luxury, like the House of Usher.

Next to this unworldly bounty, Eddie felt like a cast member of *Hee-Haw*. But at least he wasn't alone; Bill had brought a whole brigade of college friends down from Alabama so they could be frightened by that fierce rich shack. While all the Louisianans pattered around inside upon its marble floors, the Alabama people stayed huddled outside near the sumptuous fountain with its double-headed dolphin fountain.

"See those fish?" the groom had said on a brief reconnaissance foray to his native population.

They all looked at the fish floating dumbly in the fountain.

"They're not native to Louisiana. If there was to come an earthquake and the fountain cracked, those fish'd get out and eat all the native fishes."

Was that a threat or a metaphor? Eddie gazed at the trapped fish until Bill went back inside. *I feel you, my brothers*, he silently told the fish.

"You're staying through the wedding supper, aren't you?" a sudden voice came from the lower left side of Eddie.

Clay.

"Hey, Clay. Hey, I'm sorry I didn't get to say 'hey' to you earlier."

Of all the people from Alabama, Clay had changed the most and the least. He had always been a little stocky next to everyone in the sylph Rolling Stones-fan/larval stage of their youth, but now he looked far better than everyone else, muscular, tough, impervious.

"I didn't know you were coming, Eddie," Clay said.

"I didn't know you were coming, either."

"Oh, I live here now. I'm a nurse at the Oschner Clinic."

The last Eddie had heard, Clay had dropped out without graduating. Because of that, he had assumed Clay had slipped into squalor. A lot of people he knew back in college had straddled a kind of bohemian loucheness, which could go either way at any time: up to the air fern intelligentsia or back into car repair. You never knew.

"Well, that's grand. A nurse, huh."

"Yeah, I live here now. That's how I ran into Bill." He shrugged. "We get together every now and then for old times' sake."

"Neat. See, Bill asked us–a bunch of us who, you know, graduated with him–to be groomsmen. He had to act like he had his own set of friends against hers, I suppose. I haven't told them the last time I saw Bill, he bought a bag of pot from me and then split."

"Was it good stuff?"

"Ummm." Eddie was not completely pleased to see Clay. His current life was lateral, precise; he was bothered to remember that, right after graduation at some snakebrawl of a party, Clay had made a pass at him.

"The last I heard," Clay said in his placid, nurse-like way, "you were seeing Frankie. Did you all...finalize that?"

Laocoön. Eddie hadn't seen Frankie for nearly seven years. "Well, she went into a kind of major manic state back around 1980. I got a little note from her that said, 'I'm going to Atlanta,' and that's all she wrote. I think she thought she'd hook up with the B-52's."

"Atlanta." Clay nodded.

Eddie wondered if Clay felt it was Frankie who had rescued Eddie from Clay's unnatural embrace. "How about you, Eddie?" Clay said in a neutral way. "You still living in Huntsville?"

Bill must have told him. "Yep. Working in this new computer firm."

Clay looked away. "Jesus, Eddie, don't be afraid. What was it, fifteen years ago? If I had shot you then, I'd be a free man by now."

Vicki Casteel wandered up to them. She was another hillbilly from everyone's past, now married to another groomsman. "I'm havin' a nervous breakdown," she said in a loud voice.

"Why?" Eddie said politely. He was not happy to see her either.

"New Orleans is tough. I have been drinkin' since ten o'clock this morning. I feel totally out of my class."

"Isn't that pretty late in the day for you, Vicki?" Before *l'affaire* Frankie, Eddie had also dated Vicki for a couple of years.

She deliberately ignored Eddie. "Clay! Oh, my God! What are you doin' here! Last I heard you were workin' in a JiffyMart. I'm surprised you're still alive!"

Clearly she was also surprised that Clay was at this nice party.

"That JiffyMart gig was just to keep things going while I went through the first part of nursing school." Clay was still supernaturally placid.

"Did you finish?" She seemed avid to hear about Clay's failure as if it would help her feel better about herself.

"I've finished the LPN degree, but I'm still in school. I'm aiming to be a nurse practitioner."

Vicki seemed to sober up a little at that.

Eddie stepped in. "New Orleans *is* tough, Vicki."

When he had first gotten into town on Friday, he had been shocked. Over the years, he'd gotten a certain idea of New Orleans: pralines, iron balconies, beautiful old Canal Street, bars full of linen-colored light. Now from street to street the city seemed in a flux of ironies, one street full of pretty little houses gated tight as shut eyes, the next street bristling with store signs written in Tamil or Hmong. After he had checked into the Sheraton on Canal, he took a stroll down to the Quarter. It was when he reached to edge of Jackson Square that the city burst forth raw in all its elements and he was stunned.

And, as if in a dream, a young black teenager began speaking to him. "I bet you ten dollars I know where you got them shoes."

What was the guy talking about?"

"Ten dollars, man. Ten dollars." The young man must have interpreted Eddie's shock as affirmation.

"You got them shoes on Bourbon Street! Yeah, they planted right here on Bourbon Street!"

Eddie looked around. He was now surrounded by five or six of the young man's friends. "Hey, man, make good on your bet," the first man said, and the other men began to make dangerous-sounding murmurs.

He knew he looked stupefied, choiceless, but fair enough. When he forfeited the money, the young men took it and melted back into the crowd.

After that, Eddie had gone back to his hotel and sat on the bed, trying to work through the threat. The whole stupid trip was collapsing into one desire: to go back to his little apartment in Huntsville, back to his little apartment, to his little job, to the fact that he was unnoticed by that homogenized world. Being seen, being spotted made him uneasy. In his real world, the biggest threat was from his cat, Wally, who always got bored and tried to sneak outside.

But that was Friday, and this was Saturday. His sympathy for Vicki ended as soon as she opened her mouth again. "Clay, are you still gay?"

"Well, Vicki, it just won't go away. It's like skin or blood with me. Go figure."

"Behave, Vicki," Eddie said in a low voice. "Here come the rich people."

"You asshole," she hissed; then they all turned to their hosts.

The wedding supper was held at a country club that fronted out on Lake Ponchartrain. As someone, some bridal relative, drove them there, Eddie kept an eye on New Orleans. It was amazing how many identities the city could assume in just a few brief blocks. One second there was a welter of little clapboard slums full of naked toddlers holding whiskey bottles, and then great white buildings emerged new and luxurious, practically antebellum again, out of the water.

"I'm about ceremonied-out," he whispered to Clay in a low voice. "I can't wait to be free."

"What hotel are you staying at?" Clay said in a voice that seemed to be a coiled rope, but Eddie found those coils welcoming.

"I was at the Canal Sheraton, but I checked out at five. I thought I might effect an escape if I played my cards right."

"You're going to drive back now?"

"I'm more tired than I thought I would be, Clay. I guess I better see if somebody's got a spare bed back at their hotel."

"Why don't you spend the night with me?"

Laocoön, at last.

Clay turned on a couple of lamps. He had gold silk lampshades, and Eddie was distracted by their beauty; it looked like Aladdin's cave.

"Nice," he said and took Clay's hand. Then he leaned over and, helpless in his own emotions, kissed Clay on the forehead.

"Is that how this is going to be?" Clay said. His voice had that uncoiled rope in it again.

Eddie took a deep sigh. "Don't we have things to discuss?"

"How do you play this back in Huntsville?"

"I've been tested. Is that what you mean?"

"Me too. It's a professional thing here. And I always take the precautions."

"Not like it used to be."

"Not like it used to be," Clay said agreeably and kissed Eddie on the neck.

Eddie could feel Clay's tongue flicker again his neck, live as a vein. He placed his hand on Clay's chest; he could feel the warm blood coursing through Clay's body. He had no idea what was going to happen next, and he felt a sudden happiness. They were friends and cordially intertwined, and, away from the Aztec/Creole wedding festivities, Eddie had all the time in the world. He moved his hand to Clay's belt. "May I?" he whispered softly.

"There are things we'll need to use." Clay sounded almost apologetic.

"Good. I want to use them."

"They're beside my bed."

"How clever you are!" Eddie had unzipped Clay's pants; he could feel the weight of Clay's strong thick cock under his hand.

The bedroom had one complete wall of French doors or windows or whatever they were called, and the rest of it seemed lined in immaculate white cotton–a shrine to a certain medical, yet sensual tidiness.

"Trim yourself in your device," Eddie said softly. "I want to go first."

"I always use two heavy duty ones," Clay said.

When Clay was through tinkering, he lay back and Eddie leaned over him. He could smell sea and impulse, and he used everything he could to make Clay feel the same thing he himself was feeling, all the delightful sensations of Clay's impatient breathing, the pure perfume of his flesh. And the moment turned into a time that didn't tick, but floated like fire or water, and Eddie felt as if he were spinning in the stars. Meanwhile, Clay's moans became more and more intense, and then there was an explosion and Clay gasped as if he were emerging from water.

They looked at each other.

Then, after a pause, Clay said, "Now let me."

And, with a tender gesture, he freed Eddie's cock, aching now, harder than it had ever been, from its imprisoning clothing and, with a touching precision, put two rubbers on him.

Oddly enough, the condoms felt great, as if he were being cherished, protected. Clay had made placing the devices a kind of caress which naturally evolved into his rubbing Eddie's hard cock, and Eddie felt Clay caressing again, gently, and roughly, and gently and roughly. Then the moment of crisis was approaching, and Eddie leaned in and pressed his cheek hard against

Clay's while he panted just as Clay had done.

The air was calm, not tense, but Eddie felt he should say something. "That was so great. You have a...well, you have a big one. Very big and thick. My." Was that an appropriate thing to say?

"Eddie, can I ask when you turned gay? A long time ago, you indicated it was out of the question."

"Well, actually, gay snuck up behind me and made a noise, and that was when I turned."

"Ha ha. Why?"

"It's been on the agenda for a bit."

There was a pause. Eddie knew Clay was studying his next remark. Then he spoke. "So, back home, you play pretty safe?"

"I read about sex more than anything else. I have a lot of literature."

"You don't have a boyfriend."

"I nearly did at one time." Not enough Laocoön. "We drifted apart."

There was another pause.

"Eddie, would you like to take it inside you?"

"Are you joking?"

"You don't do much of that, do you?"

"I used to think about it a lot, but the things you hear these days..."

"It's the best thing ever, but..." Clay gave him a gentle little kiss on the side of his face, "but I can make it ultra safe." Somehow there was a latex glove on his hand, and he moved one finger very gently into the center of Eddie's heartbeat. "How does that feel?" Eddie said nothing, but he could feel the heat rising in his face. "Does it feel good?" Clay insisted.

"Don't stop. I've never felt anything like it."

Clay pressed a second finger in, trying to find that special place. "Give in to it."

In a few minutes, Eddie was hard again, sweating and sighing. Clay put his other hand around Eddie's cock, and Eddie reached down and patted Clay's hand, as if to urge him onward. Clay alternately squeezed

Eddie's cock and ran his thumb gently over its engorged head. Eddie could hear the city ringing around both of them. Like the city, his blood was the blood of river and wind, and then he was helpless against his own private storm and all was sensation and he went rigid with pleasure.

Clay woke him up. The air was sweet, as if it were very early. "I have to go to work, Eddie. I have this shift, see. Now you've got to go to lunch with them at Bobo LeCue's. But I'll get off at three. Meet me at the Café du Monde at 3:30. You got that?"

"Yeah. Yeah."

When he woke up again, it was eleven, and he felt absurdly refreshed. Clay's little apartment was really nice. Well, Clay was gay; that was the main reason he had a nice place. The bare old floors were warm to the touch in the early New Orleans summer, warm as flesh, and the walls were bone-colored plaster; they seemed to have a faint pink pulse in the sunlight. The apartment seemed on the verge of taking a breath.

Bobo LeCue's marked the first time Bill's friends were in the majority on that whole weekend. Over the last year or so, Eddie had developed a kind of grown-up taste for red wines. Since he ended up doing a lot of his drinking alone in his apartment (well, Wally the cat was always there), it was pleasant to eat well and drink well.

It wasn't even so very bad that Vicki was creating an almost epic standard of awfulness. "My next time out I'm marryin' a sexy man," she said with alcoholic fervor and confidence. "I've slept with most of the men at this table, so I have grounds of...to go on."

"I didn't know that," the bride said. She looked glazed and forlorn.

"I was engaged to Eddie. I still carry the picture for our engagement." She looked around. "It's back at the hotel. In a thing."

Eddie had never been engaged to Vicki. Had he?

Bill was laughing. "You should have shared this with us, Eddie."

"It was a fully nuclear secret. But, you know what, I have to meet Clay in the Quarter." He turned to the hovering waiter. "I'll need a go-cup."

Even on a dead Sunday afternoon, New Orleans was restless and lively. The city bubbled as if the Mississippi were carrying all the countries of the world in its muddy mouth. No one was working exactly, but everyone was busy, and it made Eddie cheerful. Nothing could shake this great city.

Clay was already there, standing against a wall like James Dean, only smiling.

Eddie had reached a perfect balance of alcohol in his blood.

"I didn't know if you were going to show up," Clay said.

"I can't think of what would keep me away."

"It's strange to see you as another gay man. What kept you?"

"I guess I still hadn't found what I was looking for."

"Is that true? Or a song?"

Eddie felt as if his heart had learned to play the trumpet. He laughed. "It's a song. Listen, I've decided to move here. As a matter of fact, I'm going to move in next door to you."

"Is that bullshit?"

"No, I promise. Will the landlord let me keep Wally?" He had never noticed the careful structure of Clay's face. Dimples in his chin and dimples in his cheeks–a movie star lifeguard's tanned build and look at the long lashes on those ice blue eyes. "My life is nothing but a series of zeroes and ones. I'm tired of that. I want to stay like this."

"Drunk."

"Yeah, that and gay."

"Let us go to a gay bar then."

It was called Hey Boy's, and when they walked in a man greeted them. "Clay, darling! Here's to you, Clay! Bartender, give us more huge drinks." He was an older man; he looked like a Republican cabinet member.

"Eddie, meet Glen. He was a patient of mine."

"An important one too. Heart transplant. What was it I got, an orangutan's heart?"

"Nope, it was an alligator's."

"Well, hell, Miss Carol Burnett, that explains a lot. More drinks for me and the funny girls! More and more drinks!"

Suddenly they were all sitting at a table. A black man with shaved eyebrows came over, and he and the older man tongue-kissed. In time to the kiss, there was a burst of noise from the jukebox. It sounded like somebody trying to open a drawer in an old desk. Then the noise resolved itself into a Hall and Oates song. "Your kiss is on my list," said the black man ironically to the cabinet member.

And if Eddie's blood had been perfect before, it was more perfect now. He had always vaguely associated the song with Miss 1980, Frankie. Now, in that second he forgave her; in his fantasies, she had been swimming neurotically around the interstate system of Georgia for the last seven years. Now he wanted her happy; she would trouble him no more. The worst had already happened. The eighties were about counted out, and he was here in New Orleans where a man could go directly to night at any time of the day. He looked at Clay who was looking back at him. He blinked, and they were back into the night of intimacy and warm soup of love.

"Hey, Clay," said the black man. "Are you drunk yet?"

"Well, I've got catching up to do. Plus I've got to get this one to sleep so he can drive to Alabama tomorrow and get his cat and come back here."

New Orleans, full of its clatter and burned smells and random lights, would cheer him on, New Orleans, the honey-breathing lips of America. And all Eddie had to do, to ever do, was ride the river to the future. He lay his head down on the damp table top. He was in life.

The End

Impossible Love

Kathryn L. Ramage

On a day ninety-two years ago, a young man of cherubic appearance in somewhat odd and unfashionable clothes walked up to the gates of the Duke's palace.

"May I have audience with Lord Dafythe, please?" he called up to the guards stationed on the wall above. "I've come such a very long way to see him."

Ninety-two years later...

Andemyon Lightesblood spent weeks searching the extensive library at the University of Maryesfont's College of Magic for books about wizards who had traveled through time. Everything he found, he read with voracious attention, then consulted his friend Mikha.

"Can such a thing actually be done?" Andemyon asked. "Is there a spell that can send a person into another time? I've read dozens of stories of spells used by wizards of old to view the past, and even enter it, but they might be no more than fairy-tales and not at all true."

"Oh, they are true," answered Mikha. "It has been done, but such spells require the talents of a most powerful magician."

"Could *you* do it, Mikha?"

"I don't know. I've never tried."

Mikha was the most promising magician of his generation and, though very young, already showed some remarkable powers. He was a scholar of arcane spells, which was one of the reasons Andemyon sought his help. The other reason was that the two had been close friends since Andemyon had first come to the university three years ago. Maryesfont was primarily a place for the education of women, and male students on the campus were few. Both were also students of magic, and it was only natural that they should meet and befriend each other. While Mikha was preparing for his future profession, Andemyon's interest in the subject was intellectual; he was the younger son of the Empire's premiere wizard, Yryd Lightmaster, and the only member of the wizard's family without a spark of magical aptitude. He had grown up amid magicians and their spellcraft, but he could never have asked his family for assistance with *this* problem!

Mikha, on the other hand, would understand why he wanted to do this. Andemyon was sure of that. His friend would listen to whatever he had to say and keep his secrets. Confiding in Mikha was like going to confession, without the penance that followed. Andemyon had come to think of the dark and solemn, abstemious young man as something like a priest–for, like a priest, Mikha was under strict vows of abstinence while he underwent the third purification phase of his mage's training. For seven years, he must remain chaste, never touch a drop of wine nor taste blooded meats, and keep sleepless vigils on certain nights of the year. Unlike a priest, Mikha would be free of these vows once he was tested and confirmed a wizard.

"I'd need to find the right spell," said Mikha. "The college's library is very good, but you won't find such spells here. The Sisters are rather censorious about magic they feel to be contrary to the work of God and Nature. But I wouldn't be surprised if your father has books in his collection that the Sisters don't. We can look when I go to him for my testing this summer. Where is it you want to go, Demy? Or should I say *when*?"

"To Dafythe's court, a century ago. I want to meet him as he was when he first became Duke of the

Northlands, and enter his service just as I did when I was a boy."

Mikha nodded and his mouth twisted in a small, tight smile. "I will try to perform this spell for you," he agreed, "but I must say, I don't like the idea of sending you back to the days when the old Duke was a youth so you can seduce him."

Andemyon blushed. His friend understood his motives all too well, and the hint of criticism stung. "I won't seduce him!" he protested. "I only want to know if he felt anything for me...if he could, under different circumstances." He tried to explain. "He couldn't, not as we are. Nearly a hundred years stand between us. I was only fourteen when I became his page, and seventeen when I was sent away to another part of the court, and then away from the palace entirely. I was a child even then–I didn't understand why everyone whispered and laughed about the Duke's affection for me. I didn't know why there was such haste to get me away from him. Since I've grown to see what all the fuss was about, I've wondered what truth lay behind it. Did he feel more for me than an old man's kindness? If we were to meet when he was near the same age I am now, I could find out. I won't throw myself at him, Mikha, but I must know."

His friend stared at him solemnly, and Andemyon was afraid Mikha would refuse to help. Perhaps he'd been foolish to expect otherwise. So serious a mage must disapprove the use of magic for something as frivolous as this. Magic was Mikha's profession; he'd given himself to it, heart, body, and mind, so that there was room for nothing as personal as love. Andemyon had felt that before, close friends as they were. Mikha would draw away from him and retreat into a cool aloofness whenever he became too enthusiastic or affectionate. Mikha would refuse...

Then Mikha said, "Very well, Demy. If we find the right spell, I will try it. For you."

***

The truth was that he was half in love already. There'd never been one improper word or touch between himself and his aged lord, but Andemyon fondly remembered the months he'd served as the Duke's page. He'd been one among seven young boys whose duty it was to accompany Dafythe around the court, bear his messages, and attend him in his private chambers. How many nights had he sat up at the foot of Dafythe's bed, for the Duke was frequently ill and restless and in need of company in the small hours? How often had he sung to soothe Dafythe to sleep? Before it had changed, his voice had been a sweet soprano. How many tales of magicians, taken from the books in his father's library, had he repeated to Dafythe?

Those nights were among Andemyon's most treasured memories, for they were the only time when he and the ancient Duke were alone and could talk without formality. His memories remained unspoiled, even though the courtiers had made a scandal of it once they'd noticed that Dafythe asked for him to take this duty more often than the other pageboys. When the gossip had reached the ears of the Duke's eldest son, Lord Ambris, Andemyon had been abruptly removed from Dafythe's service and they'd never been left alone together again.

Ah, but those nights! During those nights, Andemyon had told Dafythe what it was like to grow up in the house of a wizard; Dafythe in turn had told him thrilling tales of his own boyhood in the Emperor's court. They were both younger sons of great men, and that had made a bond between them in spite of the vast difference in their ages. Dafythe talked of how he'd come to the Northlands as a young prince to rule this faraway territory in his father's name. He'd made the Northlands, which had always been Andemyon's home, sound like a fabulous wilderness of tall trees and strange beasts, with only a few scattered castles, fortified towns, and villages. Dafythe himself had made it into the civilized realm it was today. He spoke of his friends of those long-ago days, gentlemen all and trusted courtly advisors, and it seemed like something out of legend, like the tales of King Arthur and his knights. As he'd listened to these stories, Andemyon had pictured the ancient Duke as a youth not much older than himself, and imagined himself at Dafythe's side.

Had it begun then? Had this idea that he might reach into the past to meet Dafythe already formed in his mind? All he needed now was a way to make it come true.

Nothing more was said for the rest of the term. He and Mikha continued their separate studies at Maryesfont and occasionally met in the young mage's rooms at the top of the library to talk, but Andemyon thought his friend had grown more reserved with him. No doubt Mikha continued to disapprove of his plans.

When summer came, they traveled together to the Lightmaster's castle, a large, empty, and solitary building on cliffs at the far end of Greenwaters Island, where Mikha would be tested. If he could prove himself a proficiently skilled magician, he would end the third phase of his training, be released from his mage vows, and be confirmed a true and full wizard.

Yryd Lightmaster, tall and austere, and surprisingly youthful himself for a wizard of such fame and power, met them on their arrival. This fabled bringer of storms, this destroyer of lesser wizards, this force of lightning and fire wrought in mortal form, smiled with very human delight at the sight of his half-grown son, and greeted Andemyon with a fierce embrace and kiss upon his tousled curls. He was more genial to Mikha than he usually was to mages who came to him to be tested.

"You needn't be afraid," the wizard promised his son as they entered the castle. "If all I've heard of this Mikha is true, he'll do very well. But you mustn't expect I will be more indulgent with him than I've been with the others, because he is your friend."

"I don't expect it, Father," Andemyon answered.

"Nor does Mikha." He turned to look over his shoulder at his friend, who was walking several paces behind them, somewhat timid since meeting Andemyon's fearsome father. "Only be fair."

"I am always fair, my child. Even if he fails, I promise you I will not harm him."

The testing of a mage was rigorous, but private, a process only those who would undergo it could know. Such magical matters were not for Andemyon, and he didn't ask what went on between his father and friend when they emerged after long hours shut up in the chamber atop the castle's highest tower, both looking weary and strained. While Mikha and the Lightmaster were occupied with their grim business, Andemyon searched through his father's books for spells that had to do with time.

Nearly two weeks after he and Mikha had come to the castle, he was in his room, studying a particularly promising tome, when he heard the patter of footsteps running along the hallway outside. As he rose from his seat at the desk, the door to his room burst open. Mikha had become pale and tense during the days of his testing, but he was smiling now, smiling as Andemyon had never seen him before.

Before the youth could speak a word, his friend caught him up in his arms and announced, "We've finished, Andemyon! I am at last a wizard!"

Then Mikha quickly set Andemyon down and recovered his composure. He withdrew into aloofness again, but this time it was because of his own unmage-like exuberance rather than anything Andemyon had done.

Andemyon smiled. "Father wasn't too hard on you?"

"Oh, no. There were times I thought..." the young wizard grew solemn as he recalled it. "He gazed into my mind, Demy, and I felt as if he could *see* everything I was or had ever done. If there'd been a flaw in my training, or if I'd let my vows lapse even once, he would have discovered it." Color appeared on his pale cheeks. "I was terrified that he would blast me to ashes But he never did. I think I surprised him. He told me himself he'd never before encountered a young magician with such strength to withstand him. If I should challenge him hereafter, when I have come into my full powers–"

"You wouldn't," said Andemyon. He knew that this was the way of wizards–even between allies or friends, there was an unending rivalry, as they constantly challenged each other to establish and maintain their places in the hierarchy of who was most powerful–but it horrified him to think that his father and closest friend would do battle one day. One or the other might be destroyed. "Mikha, promise me that you won't."

Mikha smiled at his earnestness "I can't promise you, Demy, but I think that your father and I have come to an agreement on that point, without word. Neither of us would wish harm that one whom we both love best." His cheeks colored again, and he turned his head aside to notice the book Andemyon had left open on the desk. "You've found a spell to send you to Lord Dafythe?"

"Yes. I think it's the right one." Andemyon picked up the book. "Come and tell me."

Mikha read the miniscule writing on the page. "It looks right...Andemyon, are you certain you wish to do this?"

The youth nodded. "I know you don't approve, Mikha, but I have to find out. You will help me, won't you? You won't take it back?"

"I won't take back my word," Mikha replied. "Copy out your spell, and we'll try it as soon as we are finished here."

A newly made wizard was meant to wander, to seek knowledge and experience from all the corners of the world before he was ready to challenge the elder wizards and establish his place among their ranks. But Mikha did not intend to go far on his first journey, for Andemyon was going with him. After his confirmation ceremony, in which Mikha formally took up the robes of a wizard, they left the castle and rode to the Duke's city of Pendaunzel. They took a room at an inn not far from the palace gates, but went out at sunset to leave the city and enter the woods beyond its walls.

After searching for a time in the fading light, they found a clearing within a cleft of rocks, distinctive and untouched. "This spot is exactly the same as it would've been a hundred years ago," Mikha explained. "This spell will move you through time, but not space."

"What must I do?" asked Andemyon.

"Stand there," Mikha directed, and placed him in the center of the clearing. Using a broken branch, he drew a circle in the mossy earth around the youth.

"And how do I return?"

"Come back to this same place, when you're ready. Are you ready?"

Andemyon nodded, heart beating faster now that they were actually at the point of performing the spell. Would it work? Or would he only be left looking very foolish before his censorious friend?

Mikha climbed up to perch on a large rock that loomed above the clearing, and began to recite the words of the incantation. It seemed to Andemyon that his friend's voice grew very faint, as if he were far away. The dark figure on the rock flickered and faded, then disappeared altogether.

Ninety-two years before...

A young man of cherubic appearance in somewhat odd and unfashionable clothes walked up to the gates of the Duke's palace.

"May I have audience with Lord Dafythe, please?" he called up to the guards. "I've come such a very long way to see him."

The young Duke had arrived to assume his duties only a few days before, but a number of petitioners had already gathered. People had come from all over the Northlands in anticipation of their new liege lord's arrival, and Andemyon was assumed to be one more. He gave his name, and was admitted to the palace grounds.

If he'd had any doubt that Mikha's spell had worked, the sight of the Duke's palace told him that he was truly in another time. This was not the grand array of stately buildings and cultivated parklands that he knew so well, almost a city in itself, with courtyards surrounded by long colonnades, towers that rose above the trees, and the chapel spire that seemed to pierce the sky. One day, over five hundred people would live and work here. But now, Andemyon walked up a dirt road toward the Great Hall, which sat alone on the hill–how lonely and bare it looked without its pillared portico and the two wings stretching out on either side! There was nothing else within the walls but the old castle keep and a few unimpressive outbuildings to house guards and stable horses.

He entered the Great Hall, where petitioners were waiting outside the Duke's chambers. He waited too, for what seemed like hours. At last, there came a moment when one petitioner admitted to the Duke's presence departed, and the next had not yet been shown in. The door stood slightly ajar. Summoning his nerve, Andemyon crept forward and peeked in. Dafythe had risen from his seat on the dais and was pacing before it.

Andemyon had seen paintings of Dafythe in his youth, formally posed portraits in lush purple robes that would one day hang on the walls of this same hall, but they didn't prepare him for the sight of this long-limbed young prince, all arms and legs in nervous motion. He cast aside his formal robes and was in an unadorned if well-cut and luxurious-looking tunic and hose. Dark chestnut hair tumbled loose around his shoulders. He turned suddenly, as if sensing that he was not alone; his face was all bone, the skin tanned and taut. Dafythe looked a little fretful and impatient after receiving so many of his new subjects, but his face changed at the sight of his latest visitor. When he smiled, the resemblance to his yet-unborn children and grandchildren was remarkable.

"Come in, boy," said Dafythe, and waved to dismiss the guard, who should have been keeping watch at the door but had only now returned to uphold his duty. "Are you a messenger?"

"No, my lord," the boy replied with a low bow. "I speak only for myself. I come to offer you my service. My name is Andemyon Lighteschild. I am the son of the wizard Yryd Lightmaster."

"I haven't heard his name before," said Dafythe. "I thought I knew the names of all the magicians in my father's realms. He must be a minor wizard of this land."

"He is of the Northlands, my lord," Andemyon answered, "but he will be the most powerful wizard in the world one day."

The young Duke laughed. "You have great faith in your father's abilities, my lad. What of your own? Do you intend to serve me as a court magician?"

"I'm not magical myself, Lord Duke. I thought I might act as your secretary–it appears you have great need of one–or perhaps as a guide."

Dafythe looked interested. "Guide?"

"You are new to the Northlands, my lord, and not yet familiar with our people and their ways."

"Yes, that's so," Dafythe agreed. "I've come miles over the sea at my father's bidding. He *is* the most powerful man in the world, Emperor of the greatest realm ever known. He hardly pays attention to this little part of his empire at all, so long as the taxes and proper tributes are paid. I suspect that he means to test me, or to see me out of the way for a time in this wilderness. But I mean to surprise him. I hope to make this Northland of yours a land the Emperor will be proud of. Can you aid me in this task, Andemyon Lighteschild?"

"Lord Duke, I believe I can," Andemyon replied. "If you will permit me."

He was appointed the Duke's personal aide. Within a few weeks, he was indispensable. His advice was always perfect.

"What a marvel you are, Andemyon!" Dafythe exclaimed one evening while alone with the youth in his chambers.

They'd spent the day riding around the countryside and viewing the villages near the palace. Not a formal progress–that would come later–but Dafythe was eager to see something of the land he was to rule. They'd visited Pendaunzel, the port less than a mile from the palace, where Dafythe had landed after his sea voyage. It was little more than a harbor surrounded by warehouses, some drinking houses, shops, and one shabby inn. Dafythe thought it could be more: a true "Duke's city," a place where ships from all over the world might dock, as well as a cultural and administrative center. He'd returned to the palace full of ideas and expounded on them to his smiling courtiers over dinner, and more to Andemyon afterwards. Once they'd gone to his chambers, Dafythe took up a quill and pot of ink and began to sketch it all out.

The more he saw of what the Duke was like as a young man, the more Andemyon admired him. Dafythe would never be a magnificent warrior-king like his father, but he was as great a man in his own way. He might be an intellectual and dreamer, but he had enough common sense and strength of will to see his ideas realized. As Dafythe spoke of his plans for the future, Andemyon knew how much of it would come true, and his heart beat faster with pride. At moments such as this, he was reminded of Mikha and how he and his friend used to discuss the source and purpose of magic– although the two men were nothing alike beyond a certain raw-boned lankiness and intensity. Was it the way Dafythe's eyes shone with excitement, like Mikha's, when he spoke of what was most important to him?

Encouraged by the young Duke's enthusiasm, Andemyon offered some ideas of his own: "You might cut a processional avenue from the palace gates down to the water," he suggested. "A straight road, cobblestoned and lined with trees on both sides."

Dafythe drew it in. "There must be fine buildings to either side, but I suppose those will come after the road to reach them has been made."

"They'll come up to the palace wall someday. What about a theatre? If you mean to make Pendaunzel a city of the arts as well as commerce, you must have a theatre. Bigger than the one at Maryesfont. A great O of wood and brick, open to the air at the middle with balconies all around the sides."

"Like the imperial playhouse in London?"

Andemyon had never been to London, but he knew what the Duke's Theatre would look like; he'd accompanied the aged Dafythe and his family there many times.

Dafythe drew a large circle to one side of the processional. "How do you *do* it?" he asked as he looked over the rough map of the city that was to be. "It's almost as if you read my thoughts and make my intentions clear. You see it all exactly as I do! You mayn't be a wizard, but I'm certain there's some magic in you."

Andemyon relished this praise, even though there was no magic involved beyond the spell that had brought him here. It was simply a matter of knowing his history; he could advise Dafythe to do exactly what he knew Dafythe had done.

"I sometimes think you were sent here specially to me," Dafythe continued. "An angel in answer to a prayer for aid and guidance."

"I'm no angel, my lord," Andemyon answered, smiling. "But I did come to you for my own reasons."

"Which are...?"

"To meet you. To see you, as you are, and to serve you, if I could."

Dafythe laughed. "An angel, just as I said."

They worked on his plans until a late hour of the night, and even when he at last set down his quill and flexed his aching fingers, Dafythe's eyes were still bright with excitement. "I feel as if we ought to begin work tomorrow," he said. "What trouble it seems, that I'll have to argue the merits of it for weeks before I can send a single man to lay down the first bricks."

"Your councilors will do whatever you wish. Haven't I picked them all out for you?" Andemyon was sure of this, for he well remembered the stories Dafythe had told him of these early days of his reign. He recommended councilors to be appointed to precisely the positions he knew they would occupy, and suggested exactly those plans and policies that the Duke's Council would implement. He had no desire to alter the past, only to make himself a part of it.

"So you did. We shall have to see how agreeable they are, in the morning..." As Dafythe extended his arms wide and arched his back in a stretch, he turned his head to the window. "It's nearly morning already! The night is nearly done, and I don't imagine I'll get much sleep."

This was the moment. "Shall I stay up with you, my lord?" Andemyon offered, scarcely breathing.

But Dafythe answered, "No, Andemyon. You'd better be off to bed. I've kept you up late enough with my talk."

"I don't mind it, my lord. I can see you're still restless. We can go on talking of the new city, or–or I could sing to you."

"Sing?"

"I've been told I sing very nicely."

Dafythe smiled. "I feel sure you do, as perfectly as you do everything else, But I've no need of lullabies, thank you. Go to your bed, Andemyon, and sleep."

Thereafter, Andemyon did all he could to show how willing he was to do anything Dafythe desired, without making an open declaration of love or flinging himself into Dafythe's arms–but time and again, his oblique offers were rebuffed. Dafythe seemed not to understand them. Could an intelligent man be so blind? Or was *this* his answer? Dafythe had no desires, but was simply fond of him; the young Duke valued his advice and enjoyed the companionship of someone who shared his enthusiasm for the future of the dukedom. Nothing more.

The summer drew to a close, and Andemyon grew dispirited. He must decide soon: should he summon the courage to speak, or should he admit to failure and return to his own time? He was beginning to miss the Northlands he'd grown up in, a more civilized and comfortable place than this colonial wilderness. He missed his family, and he missed Mikha. He would go home...and yet he lingered. In spite of his disappointment, he enjoyed the young Duke's company as much as Dafythe enjoyed his, and he hadn't quite given up hope.

One evening after dinner, when they were playing chess in Dafythe's chambers, a message arrived for the Duke bearing the Imperial seal. Dafythe took it away to read in private, and returned some minutes later still holding the message, its seal now broken. There was a look of distress on his face that alarmed Andemyon.

"What is it, my lord?" he asked "Bad news?" He tried to recall his history. What disaster had befallen at this date?

Dafythe shook his head and announced, "I've been informed that I am betrothed to one Lady Aline, daughter of Father's Lord High Chamberlain. It's all arranged."

"You won't marry her," said Andemyon. This wasn't a denial, but a simple statement of fact. Dafythe wouldn't marry until he was nearly fifty, and then to a noblewoman of the Northlands.

Dafythe smiled. "I've no wish to marry anyone at present, least of all someone I hardly know, but I don't see how I can refuse. It's Father's wish–and my father's wishes are orders that must be obeyed. Someone has carried tales to him, and he's decided that this is the best means to quash them."

"Tales?" Andemyon knew that there was gossip about him and Dafythe, although, to his dismay, there was no more truth to it now than there'd been in his boyhood. Even when he spent half the night in Dafythe's chambers, nothing passed between them that the entire court could not have witnessed. But the Duke's courtiers were jealous of his position and influence. Those whom he had recommended to appointments and those who had hopes were wise enough not to complain, but others, disappointed, whispered about the Duke's obviously favoring a pretty youth. And while Dafythe was oblivious to his offers, Andemyon was aware that there were gentlemen of the court, and ladies too, who would've been happy to take them up if they hadn't believed that he belonged to Dafythe exclusively. Had the stories carried so far as to reach the Emperor's ears?

Dafythe brandished his letter. "Father writes of it very frankly. If I've the misfortune to be 'buggerer of young boys,' then I should have the decency not to flaunt my scandalous behavior with my 'catamite,' but conceal it and get married as soon as possible before I completely disgrace myself. I'm to get rid of you, or at least, I'm not keep you so close by me that it causes this sort of talk. Perhaps he's right, Andemyon, for your sake as much as mine. You're too fine a young man to become the object of vile gossip because of my affection for you."

"But I don't care what they say," Andemyon answered honestly. "I wouldn't mind the gossip, my lord, even if it were true." Stepping forward, closer to the Duke, he made the bravest move he had dared so far; it might be his last chance. "Dafythe, I wish it were." And he flung himself.

For an instant, Dafythe's mouth was against his– then Dafythe's hands were on his shoulders and he was being held away at arm's length. To Andemyon's relief, Dafythe didn't appear angry at his audacity, nor disgusted, but the young Duke's eyes were sad.

"Oh, my dear Andemyon. I was afraid it was so. I've grown accustomed to people who bow-and-scrape and make up to me because I am a prince, but no one has ever regarded me as if *I* were wonderful myself. That it should be a boy like you! You are like no one I've met before. You've been more help to me than you realize during these last difficult months. I don't know what I'd have done without you. But you must see that it is impossible. I can't love you as you'd like."

Andemyon stepped away from the light grip on his shoulders, contrite and red with embarrassment. "My deepest apologies, my lord Duke. Please forgive my presumption. I won't make such a fool of myself again." With a bow, he stepped backwards toward the door.

Dafythe still looked pained. "Andemyon–"

But the young man mumbled a plea to leave his lord's presence and exited without waiting for an answer. Dafythe did not follow him.

When he left the Duke, Andemyon went to his own chambers to change into the clothes he had arrived in. He left a note of resignation and farewell where it would be found, and took nothing away with him. Once it was dark, he left the palace and returned to the woods, as Mikha had told him to do when he was ready to end this experiment.

He found the same clearing where Mikha had cast the spell and stepped into its center. He had no sense of the spell being uncast; there was only a shift in the soft light, as if the moon had abruptly changed its phase and place in the night sky, and the trees around him were different; some slender trunks had grown mighty, and others had gone. Mikha was seated on the large rock at the edge of the clearing, where Andemyon had left him.

"How long have I been gone?" he asked.

"No time at all," Mikha answered, and climbed down from his perch. "As far as I observed, you never left the circle–only flickered away for a moment, like a blink of the eye. Did it work? What happened?"

"Your spell worked wonderfully," Andemyon told him. "I was at Dafythe's court for months, served Dafythe as a young man...but nothing happened. It ended no differently in the past than it did–would–when I was a boy. I sent myself away again, for the sake of my Duke. But I know now that Dafythe doesn't care in that way for me."

"That's exactly what you wanted to find out."

Andemyon sighed. "Yes, but I'd hoped to find out something different."

Together, they walked silently back to Pendaunzel. The city was large and well lit, with broad, paved streets and a straight, tree-lined avenue, the Duke's Parade, that stretched from the gates of the palace to the harbor. A number of people were out and about, which was odd at so late an hour, and both young men overheard a certain nervous, hushed murmuring that they hadn't noticed earlier in the day. At the inn, they heard the news: Duke Dafythe had fallen ill and wasn't expected to live through the night.

A young man walked up through the crowd awaiting news at the palace gates, and called up to the guards on the wall above: "I've come to see the Duke, one last time. Will you let me in?"

Since Andemyon was known to the guards, they did not bar his entrance but admitted him to the palace grounds and escorted him up to the Duke's residence on its hill. Dafythe's eldest son, Lord Ambris, who was just outside Dafythe's chamber door in whispered conversation with a group of courtiers, looked extremely surprised when he saw the young man approach. "Andemyon Lightesblood? How came you here so swiftly?"

"I was in Pendaunzel when I heard my lord Duke was ill," Andemyon said simply. "Is it so bad as they say in the city?"

"It is," the Duke's son confirmed grimly. "A matter of hours, no more."

"May I see him, please?" Even though Ambris had been the one to investigate the rumors involving his father's favorite page and prove them false, he had also been the one who'd arranged to send Andemyon away to Maryesfont to prevent further scandal. It was possible that he would bar Andemyon from seeing the Duke, even tonight.

But Lord Ambris said, "It's fortunate you happened to be so near. Father's been asking for you. I wouldn't have sent for you at the university, but since you are here, you must come in. Your presence cannot harm him now, and may be of comfort."

He brought Andemyon into Dafythe's bedchamber, where the Duke lay. Doctors and courtiers and other members of the Duke's family were gathered; they stared at the young man as he entered, for they all remembered the circumstances under which he'd been sent from court, but Andemyon had no mind for them. His gaze was fixed upon the figure on the bed–the long ash-white hair, the ancient face more pinched and wrinkled than when he'd last seen the aged Dafythe five years ago. But in that very old face he could detect the features of the young Duke, and when Dafythe opened his eyes, they were just the same.

"Demy..." Dafythe held out a hand, and Andemyon came to stand beside the Duke's bed to take it; the bones of the fingers were like twigs, and the skin frighteningly cool to the touch. The grip on his own hand was so light he could pull away easily if he wished to.

"I'm here, my lord Duke," he said, and squeezed the fragile fingertips gently.

"I was thinking of you, my dear...remembering. When I first saw you, you reminded me of another youth I knew, long ago. Such a lovely boy. That same look of an angel sent to aid and guide me. Did I ever tell you of him? No. He was only here for a little time, that first summer after I was made Duke. It was all his doing...all

56

of this. My palace. My city. My dukedom. It wouldn't be as it is now, if not for him. I've thought of him often since you came to serve me. The same face. The same name. Lightesblood. Lighteschild. A wizard's son. There is only you, isn't there, Demy? Only one boy."

This might sound like nonsense to anyone else who heard the Duke's soft-spoken words, drawn in and out on each labored breath, but Andemyon understood it perfectly. "Yes," he answered, "there is only me. I had to leave, for your sake."

"Ah." The Duke's mouth moved into a faint smile. "No, we couldn't have a scandal. You went away so suddenly. I never could find where you'd gone. I searched all the Northlands, but it was as if you'd never existed. I wanted to tell you. I can now, when it doesn't matter. If I could have loved you, my Andemyon..." The Duke shut his eyes. The grip on Andemyon's hand loosened, and Dafythe's fell to the bed. His physicians pushed forward to attend him, and Andemyon was driven back from the bedside. He didn't protest, but retreated to sit out of the way and wait for the end, which came within the hour.

The bells of the chapel rang to announce the Duke's death as Andemyon left the palace; the bells of the city's churches took up the peal. He could also hear the sounds of the crowd beyond the main gate mourning, for Dafythe was well beloved by his people. His death was the end of an era. Who could remember a time before Dafythe had ruled over them? He'd made the Northlands what it was, and it wouldn't be the same now that he was gone. Tears rolled down Andemyon's own cheeks at the memory of the Duke he had known, both as a young man and old.

Once outside the palace gates, he was surprised to find that Mikha had waited for him. "I'm sorry, Demy," said his friend. "I know more well than anyone what Lord Dafythe was to you."

Andemyon nodded, accepting this condolence. "I

feel as if I've lost him twice in the same day." He blotted his tears with the back of his hand. "He did love me, Mikha. He told me so. He knew who I was, that I was the same Andemyon he'd known ages ago. He was fond of me as a boy, because he remembered me...before." They began to walk back down the Duke's Parade toward the inn. According to Dafythe, *he* had made this, formed the past by entering it. But he'd only advised the young Duke to create what he knew would be one day, repeating Dafythe's own plans to him. Surely they hadn't been *his* ideas to begin with? "I understand now. It wasn't the great gap of age or time that separated us–it was his duty. Whatever he felt for me in his heart, nothing could ever have come of it, not in the past any more than today. A prince can't choose where to love. He doesn't have that freedom. That's what he meant when he said it was impossible."

They went into the inn. Daylight wasn't many hours away, but Andemyon was exhausted and heavy of heart. The bells were still ringing for Dafythe. At the foot of the steep, narrow stair that led up to their room, he leaned against his friend's shoulder for comfort, but at the touch he felt Mikha stiffen and draw away from him. In their room, Andemyon quickly took off his shoes and tunic and, in shirt and hose, climbed into the room's single bed. He looked back at Mikha, who was still standing fully clothed.

"Aren't you coming to bed?"

"No." Mikha sat down in a chair near the door and settled as if he intended to remain there the rest of the night.

"But you must be as weary as I am." He knew how spellcasting taxed a magician's strength, and Mikha had cast a very powerful spell for his sake this night.

"I'm not," his friend insisted. "I'm used to long vigils of wakefulness. You need to rest more than I do, Andemyon. Go to sleep."

Andemyon was at first hurt by this rebuff, but he cast a curious glance or two at his friend before he slept.

Two months later...

One rainy afternoon at the end of the summer–a summer that seemed twice as long to Andemyon, and not only because of the months he'd spent in the past–the young man heard the thump of boots on the stairs that led up from the College of Magic's library, then a knock on his door. He was surprised; his room here under the eaves was a solitary place where few visitors called. He rose from his work to see who it could be.

"Mikha!" Andemyon hadn't seen his friend since they'd parted the morning after Dafythe's death. Mikha had gone on his wanderings in the wilderness to the north, and Andemyon had stayed to attend the Duke's funeral before returning to the university to resume his studies. "How did you know to find me here?" he asked as he stepped back from the door to admit his friend.

"I was told you'd taken my old room," Mikha explained.

"It was vacant. The librarian needed an assistant, and someone had to look after your things." Andemyon indicated the belongings the former mage had left behind. "After all, you might want them again someday."

"As a matter of fact, I did want one or two books of mine..." Mikha glanced at the papers left lying on the floor before the hearth, where Andemyon had been sitting. "But I see you also make use of them."

"I've been reading your notes on our old experiments. Do you remember how I sought to discover the source of a magician's power?"

"Yes, of course I do. I'm glad to see you're carrying on with it, Demy. It will be of the greatest importance to all scholars of magic someday. Since I've been away, I've often thought of this room, and of you and I here." He fell silent, listening to the rain pattering on the roof.

Mikha had been speaking with his usual reserve; as a well-trained magician, his poise and self-command were nearly impenetrable to one who didn't know him well, but Andemyon thought he detected an almost wistful note in his friend's voice as he recalled the hours they'd spent together in this secluded place at the top of the library. When their eyes met, Mikha looked at him with an intensity that was much more than wistful and made him feel suddenly shy.

"I've missed you, Mikha," he said impulsively. "I would've gone with you on your travels, if you'd asked me."

"I thought it best not to," answered Mikha. "You were so grieved over Lord Dafythe's death. It was better you come back here."

"Yes, perhaps that *was* right," Andemyon sighed. He didn't meet Mikha's gaze. "I needed a peaceful and familiar place to return to, to recover from my sorrows and to think." During these past weeks, he'd spent plenty of time alone with his thoughts, and he'd come to understand a great many things. "But there was another reason you didn't wish me to accompany you, wasn't there?"

"What do you mean?"

"It wasn't my sorrow for Lord Dafythe, but my love for him. It pained you to be near me while I was still thinking of him, because *you* love me, Mikha."

This quiet statement was enough to ruffle the young wizard's composure. Mikha gaped at him. "How–? When did you know?"

"I guessed it was so on the night he died," Andemyon explained. "I kissed Dafythe once, in the past, and he held me away from him in the same way you always do when I draw too close. I used to believe that meant you disliked it, but it wasn't so. You held me away for the same reason he did: I was too dangerous to you. Too great a temptation. A mage must be even more careful than a Duke." He looked suddenly up into his friend's eyes. "I'm not wrong, am I?"

"No," Mikha admitted. "No, you aren't wrong."

"You never told me."

"How could I?" Now that his secret had been discovered, the words came quickly. "A mage has no business falling in love, especially not with an innocent young boy. It was the worst trial of my will I have had to endure. I didn't dare speak. The very moment at which I saw you might understand how I felt was the same moment when I saw you were already in love with someone else."

Andemyon bowed his head. "My lord Dafythe."

"He was a hero to you. I had no hope of comparing with your dream of him. I thought that in time you'd grow out of your infatuation, but you are such a determined scholar! Once you learned that it was possible to travel into the past to meet him as a young man, you searched everywhere for that spell."

"Yet you helped me to find it. You agreed to send me to him."

"You would've found it yourself eventually. I knew you wouldn't rest until you did, or else you'd go on dreaming after him. I thought it better not to stand in your way and allow you to find out...what you did find out."

"You *knew* how it would end?"

"I knew that, whatever happened, you couldn't remain in that other time for long."

"No," he had to agree. He'd seen that for himself long ago: if he'd been successful, even the briefest tryst between Dafythe and himself would have brought ruin to the young Duke. He might have altered that same history that he'd desired to enter in ways he could never imagine. "I couldn't stay. I'd have to return...to you?"

Mikha laughed. "Oh, I'm not so presumptuous as *that*! I didn't come back to find out if you'd gotten over your grief for Lord Dafythe–only because I couldn't stay away any longer. I had to see you. I know that you've looked upon me as a friend, no more. I've no reason to expect you to consider me, even now..." But the hopeful look in his eyes betrayed him.

"I didn't when I saw you last," Andemyon answered

honestly. "One doesn't think of a mage as a man like any other..."

Could he think of him in that way now? As his grief over Dafythe receded, Mikha was more often on his mind. He couldn't deny it. He *had* missed Mikha these past long weeks; he hadn't realized how much until now. Was he ready to accept that this friend he'd always considered untouchable was someone he could love? Yes, that was possible.

He stepped closer, and for once Mikha did not draw away. As they stared at each other, the only sound was the drumming of the rain. The university around them might not have existed, for they felt miles away from anything beyond this little room. Tentatively, Andemyon placed his hand on Mikha's cheek.

Their first kiss was rather clumsy, and it was followed by cautious, chaste little dabs that missed as often as they struck true, but that fell more rapidly and grew more soft and wet–until Mikha caught him up suddenly with a delighted laugh. Andemyon had only seen him like this once before, on the day when Mikha had been confirmed a wizard. All his careful guards were down; for the moment he was not a magician, but simply a happy young man.

"You don't know how long I've wished for this, Demy," he said. "You've made it so difficult for me to keep my vows these last years!"

"Fortunately," Andemyon answered, matching Mikha's laughter, "a mage does not have to keep his vows forever." He knew certainly that Mikha hadn't yet broken his vows and had even less experience in these matters than *he* did. But they were intelligent young men, willing to experiment, and they would soon find their way together.

The End

The Unsent Letter

Chad Denton

As I write this, I am thinking of you reading this and being disgusted enough to never call me again, to never even think about me except as an unpleasantly eccentric footnote in your biography. Oh, you are compassionate and open-minded and all those things the sort of twentysomething who cries (just a little) when he listens to Bob Dylan's *Masters of War* is, but we live in a time and a place where these things are not always understood, even by compassionate, open-minded men.

I don't want to think like that. Instead I choose to imagine you reading the letter again and again, the words infecting you with a sleepless night. I want to think that by writing this I transcend the repulsive barriers of gender and sexuality, that love triumphs in the way that it does in the most stupidly sincere of romance novels and soap operas. I see it now, as I write this, you clutching the letter in one hand, you dialing my number with the other. Then we will have so much to discuss, all to the point of thick tears and wet, sloppy "I love yous."

How would you feel if I admit to you now that I remember every single second of our first meeting? You were lurking at the edges of Lucas' party, cornered in conversation with an Art History Ph.D. student. You dropped deep, loud "hm-hmm's" at every pivotal point of the conversation, which caught my attention and awakened my neurotic tics. I looked for the sore spot and saw you, leaning precariously against a chair with a tight collared shirt that hinted at your soccer player's build. Even with your strong voice rising above and cutting through the crowd's chatter, you caught my attention only for ten seconds.

Then, with the sort of casualness that I saw as almost inhuman, you walked up to me and asked if I was a friend of Lucas' or Mary's. What started as a nervous, overextended explanation that I was friends with both of them from college somehow turned into a mournful conversation about the rise of the religious right to an analysis of the differences between British and American televised sci-fi to summaries of our families and backgrounds. How I made it that far doesn't require me to guess. It was your strange, supernatural ability to convince without a single word even the terminally shy that you are utterly sincere in your interest.

I hope you are still reading, even though it should be clear where I am going and what I wanted from almost the beginning. Perhaps you are confused, but just under all that there is also some intoxicating anticipation.

It was just before we departed at the door of Lucas' townhouse that you asked me two questions in machine gun succession: if I would like to try Vietnamese food (I gave an enthusiastic yes, although most East Asian cuisines and I were often at loggerheads) and if we could exchange numbers. Having experienced a long string of blind dates arranged through the magic of the Internet, the novel thrill of having a date that came pre-interested sustained me through the next two days.

The same conversational momentum we achieved at the party was no fluke. Still, the most physical contact we achieved was you all too briefly squeezing my hand at one point in the evening. Toward the end of the second date, a quasi drunken late night at a mini golf course, we hugged and despite myself I managed to score a kiss on the neck. By the third date, you snaked your arm around my waist, but nothing more. It was enough; in fact I know it would be enough.

For the fourth date you invited me to you house for a dinner you would prepare yourself, some Indian rice dish you were strangely proud of fishing off the Internet. It was the first time I saw you dressed up: khakis and a buttoned shirt. Perhaps you were truthful when you explained that you had a meeting with your Ph.D. program advisor and had not changed, but I prefer to think it was a subconscious effort to underscore the evening's importance. Nonetheless, our talk over rice, chicken, and white wine was light and harmless, at least until you started playing Janis Joplin and wanted to dance.

It was at that precise second I balked. All my life I had been deprived of the need to dance. Also, I still bore the usual emotional scarring of the awkward child who was starved for athletic talent from birth. Ah, thank God you assured me that you could teach me! And that you half dragged me out of the kitchen and in front of your stereo system.

We danced to 1970s rock music and Mahler and Depeche Mode and Tchaikovsky and Neko Case. An hour went by and I had rested my head against your chest. I felt your lips press after my forehead, followed right away by the words I had hoped to hear for weeks, "I love you." I repeated them, refusing to degrade their value by adding the customary "too." Afterwards there was silence; we had reached that mystical primal equilibrium where language itself is crude and unnecessary.

It was the ideal time to kiss, and in the story that unfolds again and again in my mind we did. Trapped in two steel arms, pulled close by gravity, our lips collided. It didn't matter if it was the influence of alcohol or the clumsy intimacy of our dance; all that mattered were the possibilities that were now revealed as our bodies pressed together and our love hit the same pace.

Right now, I realize it has been exactly one year since you married Mary, which is rather silly since the picture of you and her that I received just the other day is still on my desk. After all, maybe I am writing this so

I can have something tangible to keep for myself, a missive from another, better and fairer world.

What would you say, what would you do if you had read this? I do not know. I do not wish to know. And I know now that I will never know.

For always,

Your never-to-be lover.

The End

Finding Courage

Gail Marlowe

Why did the man I couldn't take my eyes off have to be so old?

I couldn't go over to him.

So he was in the Gay and Lesbian Studies section of Borders and reading a book he'd picked up from a shelf there–that didn't mean he was gay. Maybe he had a gay son or nephew or friend, or maybe he was looking at a book about lesbians because his daughter was one, or maybe he was just curious. And even if he was gay, he wore his suit as though he wore one all the time and liked it, so he was probably a professor or a businessman or someone uptight I'd never get along with.

And he was too old for me. He was probably my dad's age.

No, I couldn't go over to him and strike up a conversation. I couldn't ask him to have coffee with me. And I definitely couldn't ask him to have sex with me, even though I wanted to.

Every time I had been attracted to a guy, all through high school and all through college and now when I had a real job and made real money, he ended up being someone I couldn't go after. No, *wouldn't* go after.

I was sick of it.

Why couldn't I find an attractive guy and just see if he was into guys? Could it be that hard?

Well, yeah, it sure seemed to be. I'd known since I was a kid and thought that Batman and Superman were hot, not Catwoman or Supergirl, that I preferred guys, and I knew now I wanted to have sex with a guy, but I couldn't get up the courage to approach any guys.

Pitiful. That was me.

I moved to get a better angle while staying where I was pretty sure he couldn't see me, but I still couldn't see the cover of the book. Then the man in the suit tucked the book under his arm with the other books he was carrying and strode toward the register. Damn. Now I'd never know what he'd been reading.

I watched him as he bought his books. No, I wasn't going to go up to him and see if he wanted to have coffee with me or anything else. I was too much of a coward. But I was going to drink him in and later, when I was home, I'd imagine him watching me as I jerked off, and maybe even imagine his hands working my cock instead of my own.

Really pitiful.

He left the store without a look around or back. I took a deep breath, then another and another, and felt my cock start to soften. Then I marched over to the Gay and Lesbian Section and pulled out the first book that caught my eye, titled "The Joy of Gay Sex." I started browsing through it and was hard again almost immediately. Wow. Those pictures...I shivered. Why had I waited so long to check this section out? Because I'd been scared of doing anything in public that might show I was gay, since all my life I'd heard from my father, my uncles, my cousins, and most of the people I knew too many jokes about gay guys and how unmanly they were. Well, no more. I was a man, no matter who I wanted to go to bed with, and I was definitely buying this book.

I closed the book and scanned the titles of the other books in the section. Maybe I could find one that would help me get over my issues about approaching men, give me some tips, anything. Just because I was ordinary looking on a good day and shy and wore big, dark-framed glasses didn't mean I had to be alone forever, did it? I hoped not. I really wanted to find someone to do some of those things the pictures demonstrated.

Hell, I was going to find someone. Weren't there

gay bars somewhere around? I was in Boston, for god's sake. Men married men here. There had to be gay bars, and they'd have to advertise. I'd seen free papers in Harvard Square. I'd go there and pick up some and see if they had any ads aimed at gay men, like me.

I was sick and tired of being a coward.

I skimmed through a few books and picked out two that looked interesting, put them on top of "The Joy of Gay Sex", and carried them toward the registers. Thank goodness I wasn't so hard now.

There was a line–should I flip open one of the books and start reading? No, that wouldn't be a good idea–it wasn't that long a line and it would probably start moving just as I got to a good part. I'd use the time to think about where I'd go next. Somewhere with coffee was a given. Coffee was good. Wait, this Borders had a café. I could sit there and have coffee and read. I'd look for the free papers later, on the way home.

"Hey." I blinked. "Hey. I'm open here. I'll ring you up."

The voice came from one of the further registers, which had been closed but now had a guy standing there.

Oh god.

Forget about the man in the suit. This guy was seriously gorgeous–like Apollo or some other Greek god, with his short blond hair glinting in the light and his smile and his warm green eyes and his face and his...everything. He looked like he was about my age, and he was smiling at me.

Probably only because I was a customer, but still...it didn't seem that way.

I moved over to his register. I was next in line, after all.

He was still smiling at me.

I put the books down. I would not apologize for them. I would not explain. It was my business what I bought. I'd come in after work to look at books, and I'd found some to buy. He could think whatever he liked about me. I didn't care.

He grabbed the top one as I was digging out my wallet. "Oh, this is good. I love it."

He loved it? The book about being shy and gay and living with that and finding guys?

I handed him my Borders card. "You've read it?" My voice came out in a squeak, and I wanted to sink through the floor.

He scanned the barcode. "Yup. Lots of good advice."

He'd read it. I wanted to ask if it was because he was gay too, but that was just too stupid. Maybe he had a brother who was gay or a cousin or a close friend.

He scanned the other books. "You have good taste. Nice to see that. If after you read these, you'd like some more recs, let me know. I've read a lot."

Well, he sounded like the right person to ask about gay stuff, like bars. It wouldn't hurt to try, right? Right. I'd decided not to be a coward any more. Might as well start now.

He told me the total, and I handed him my credit card. "You mind answering a question?"

He swiped it and looked right at me. "Fire away."

"I want to find a bar where–" I swallowed. If he turned on me now, it would...I couldn't think about that. He was smiling at me, and he'd been friendly, and he'd made me feel safe talking to him. I was going to trust him. "Where I can meet guys who like guys."

He nodded and handed me back my card. "Yeah, I can tell you the names of some good places." He wasn't going to turn on me. Oh god yes, thank you. "Listen, I've got a break coming. If you'll hang around, I'll join you in a half-hour at most."

"I'll wait in the café."

"Sounds great." He grinned and pushed the receipt at me. "But sign that first, please." I did. "See you in a little while," he glanced at the receipt, "David."

His voice saying my name made me feel warm all over. "You're sure?"

He slid the books into a bag. "We guys who like guys got to stick together. Plus," his voice lowered, "you're cute."

"Me?"

His smile widened. "You."

I took the bag and floated through the store back to the café. He liked guys too. He was coming over to talk with me. He thought I was cute.

I ordered a decaf mocha and took it and my books to one of the small tables. Maybe after some coffee, I'd calm down and be able to read.

He probably just said I was cute to be nice because I knew perfectly well that I wasn't cute. And he was just going to talk to me because he saw my books and felt sorry for me. Yes, that had to be it.

And really, no way he'd been flirting with me. There was no reason to believe anything so ridiculous, even though I wanted to so much. He was so handsome.

We'd talk for the length of his break, if I was lucky. He might decide he had better things to do than talk to some guy who didn't know anything much, and why shouldn't he? After all, I wasn't anything special, and he was. But if he did stay...I shook myself out of my thoughts. Whatever happened, he'd go back to work when he needed to, I'd finish my coffee and leave when I was ready to, and that would be that.

Unless...

I closed my eyes and breathed.

I had to stop this. So he was gay. Or maybe he was bisexual. It didn't mean he was into *me*.

"Hey, David."

I opened my eyes, and he was standing there, holding a big cup of coffee, smiling down at me, so much better looking than any man, ever. I was really glad I hadn't gotten up the courage to approach the man in the suit earlier.

"I'm glad you're still here. I was afraid you might get bored and decide to take off, so I got Kim–she's my boss–to let me take my break now."

He had no idea there was no way I'd have left when he'd promised to come talk to me. "That was nice of her." Thank god my voice didn't squeak again. I managed to get my mocha to my lips and drink.

"Yeah, she's a nice person. Can I sit down?"

I nodded, and he slid into the chair next to mine, took the lid off his coffee, lifted it to his lips, and drank, then set it down. His sleeves were rolled up so I could see his muscles as he moved, and the hair on his arms caught the light and shone. I couldn't take my eyes away from him.

"So, you want to know about gay bars."

I could feel I was turning red. How could he say that so casually? "Well, yes."

"I could give you some addresses and opinions, but the better way would be for me to take you to some. How about tonight? I'm here till eight."

He wanted to take me to gay bars? And he wanted to go tonight? Wow. That was fast. I hadn't bargained on that, but it would be stupid of me to turn down such a generous offer.

"Thank you. That's nice of you." It would be easier not going alone, although I'd bet he'd get all of the attention. But maybe that would be best for my first time. I could watch him and the other men interact and figure out later what I'd feel comfortable doing and which bar I'd feel comfortable doing it at. Then the next time I'd go by myself and maybe even find someone.

"Nope, not nice at all." He stared right at me, smile gone. "If you go by yourself to any gay bar I know, some smart guy'll scoop you up and I'll never get a chance with you."

"You want a chance with me?" How? He'd just met me. I wasn't repulsive, but I wasn't handsome like him. He could get any guy he wanted, I was sure of that. Was he just being nice? It was likely. Or he was just trying to bolster my confidence. I needed a minute to decide what to do next, so I reached for my coffee, then stopped when I felt how my hands were shaking. He reached over and took them in his. I liked how warm and strong his fingers felt.

"Yeah, I do." He frowned and looked down at his coffee. "But hey, if that's not good for you, fine. I'll give you some addresses and some tips if you want them. It's just, you smiled at me, and I thought, hey, he looks interesting and interested and really cute, so I'll see what comes out of it if I make a move."

He started to pull his hands away, but I wouldn't let go. "No, that sounds fine. I'd like you with me." I didn't recognize my voice, all husky and needy, but he was looking at me again, and I liked that. "How about dinner first?" I didn't know if I was going to drink or not at whatever bar he took me to, but it made sense to have something in my stomach. And dinner with him would be like a date.

His smile came back. "I like that idea." He squeezed my hands, then let go, and this time I let him. "You gonna hang around here or come back? Or do you want me to meet you somewhere else?"

I glanced at my watch to see that it was six-thirty. "I'll stay here." Maybe I'd get another mocha. I had books to read after all, and no reason to travel home and then back again.

"Wish I could leave now, but I can't." His voice was husky too. "I hope the time goes by fast, David."

"Me too, Jamie."

"You know my name?" He sounded surprised.

"It's right there on your name tag. You know, the one you're wearing on a red cord around your neck." I couldn't help smiling.

He laughed. "Right, so it is. What an ultramaroon." He stood. "Time to get back to work."

"Don't work too hard, Jamie. I'll be here, waiting for you." I smiled and hoped he took my comments as the flirting I meant them to be.

His green eyes gleamed, and I decided that yes, I'd managed to get my point across for once. "Don't worry about that. I'll make sure to do easy stuff. I don't think my brain's working as well as it usually does. Got this cute guy on my mind instead of inventory and barcodes." He put his hand on my shoulder and squeezed. "Look through your books and see if there's anything you want to try out–sorry, shouldn't assume– ask me about later," he said softly, then lifted his hand and headed back to the store.

My shoulder was tingling, and I couldn't stop smiling. What a great idea. I'd make a list, and maybe I would get to try something out with him.

I made a short list and read it over while I drank the rest of my decaf mocha, then ordered a plain decaf. I liked coffee and chocolate together, but one was enough.

The list sounded stupid. I hadn't done anything, I was an ignorant idiot, and Jamie would figure that out as soon as we talked for more than a few minutes and want nothing more to do with me.

Well, I could fix this. I'd write a note for him, saying I'd changed my mind, leave it with someone else, get out of there. He'd shrug and never give me another thought and find someone else. I wouldn't come here again. There were other bookstores I could go to.

What was I doing? I'd told myself I'd stop being a coward.

I took a deep breath. I'd wanted a guy for years and years and years and now that I'd found one who wanted me too, I was going to run away? Hell no. I didn't want to leave. I wanted to see what might happen with Jamie. I'd come this far, so why not keep going? All I had to do was stay, so I'd stay.

I stood and reached for the empty coffee cups and napkins to throw them away. Being courageous was hard. But it was more rewarding than being scared all the time.

"Hey, David. Are you going to be hungry for dinner after all that coffee?"

It was him, smiling at me again, and I was glad I'd decided to stay.

I smiled too. "Yes. Does pizza sound good to you?"

His smile broadened. "Yeah, and I know a great place. We can either walk there or take the T."

"I'd rather walk." It had been warm enough this morning that I'd decided not to bring a jacket with me, and it was June, so it wasn't going to be cold now.

"Good. I like walking." He gestured toward the store. "I'd better get back to work. I'm shelving books. Hope I'm putting them in the right places."

"I hope so too." I reached out and touched his hand. "You'll be done soon?"

"Yeah."

"That's good news." My voice was huskier than I'd ever heard it. "I'll read a little more."

"Yeah, you do that." His voice was husky too, and he looked at me like he'd like to throw me down and kiss me or something. No one had ever looked at me like that before. "Too bad I wore these brand new jeans today. Anyone can tell I'm turned on."

Of course I glanced down, then flushed. God, those jeans were tight!

He laughed softly. "Sorry. Couldn't resist. I really will go now."

And he turned away, flashing me one more smile, and went back to the store.

I sat down again. I'd have to wait until I wasn't so hard to use the restroom. Right now it would be no use at all.

It did not help that I couldn't take my eyes off his ass. Wow. I really wanted to see him out of those jeans, and that shirt, and find out how his skin felt and tasted, and feel his hands on me...

Definitely not the time to open any of my new books.

Still looking at Jamie's ass, I made myself think of one number, then another, then a third, and added them, then added another, and so forth. Numbers. They'd help me get myself back under control.

It was forty-five long minutes before he was finished, and I was more than ready to leave when he showed up again with that drop-dead gorgeous smile.

"Okay, let's get out of here." He took off his name tag and stuffed it into his shirt pocket, then slung the jacket he was carrying over his shoulder. "You still want pizza?"

"Yes, if it's good pizza."

"It's really good pizza. Great vegetarian choices too, if that's how you go."

I shook my head. I liked meat just fine, and I wasn't that picky. I just wanted some food, and then we'd go to at least one gay bar, and then...I didn't know. Would he suggest we go to his place? Would he want to go to mine? Would he see some good looking guy at the bar and decide he could do much, much better than me?

"Hey." His hand was on my shoulder again, and it felt warm and reassuring. "You're freaking out, right?"

It must be written all over my face, not that I was surprised. I wasn't good at hiding anything. I nodded.

"Don't. We'll have some pizza. We'll talk there. Then we'll have a drink or two at this quiet bar I know, at least it's quiet during the week." He gave me a small smile. "I don't know what then. I mean, I know what I'd like–you in my bed–but I don't know if that'll be right for you. Maybe next time, if you give me a next time."

He wanted me in his bed? He was worried about *me* giving him a next time? What did he see in me? And did I really care considering I was getting everything I could have ever hoped for? Hell no. I was finding it hard to breathe, but I managed to speak. "Okay. We'll see how it goes. And a next time sounds good to me." But maybe he wouldn't want it after this time. Still, he'd said it, and that counted for something.

I couldn't help looking at his jeans again. Yes, he was erect again, or was it still?

I tore my eyes away and looked at his face. He was smiling, and I smiled back. "I like how you look."

"I like how you look too, David. Glasses and all."

I loved how he said my name. "I have to wear these."

"I wasn't making fun of you. I really like how you look in those. You look smart and cute. Really cute, like Clark Kent. I've always had a thing for him."

He'd just compared *me* to Clark Kent?

"You know who he is, right?"

"Of course I know who he is." I was going to tell him about my comics collection, then remembered that a lot of people thought comics were for kids. I could tell him later, maybe.

"Good, although it would have been fun to tell you about him."

It would have been fun to hear how he'd tell the story. Maybe I'd ask him later to humor me. "Superman is one of my favorite superheroes." Damn, I'd used the present tense. Well, it wasn't illegal to like superheroes, and he'd started it, anyway.

"Yeah, me too." He got a dreamy look in his green eyes. "Wouldn't it be great to fly?"

"Yeah." I was finding it hard to breathe, with him giving me that look again like he wanted to throw me down and kiss me.

He blew out a breath and the look was gone. "Let's get out of here, okay? I'm hungry."

"Oh, sure." I grabbed my bag with my books. I'd been here long enough.

"It's about a ten-minute walk, but it's worth it."

"I like walking." Especially with him beside me. Good thing we weren't going where anyone would know me–no one would believe we were friends. He looked too good for that.

"That's how you keep in good shape, right?" His eyes traveled up and down me. "I can tell that even with clothes on."

I was blushing and glad we were out of the store.

"Thanks. I have a treadmill I work out on at home." I had some weights too, but I didn't want to sound like I was boasting.

He turned right as we left the building. "I go to a gym, or I try to. I get lazy. I like sleeping in and I like going home after work and collapsing on the couch with the TV on." He grinned. "Maybe you could join too, and we could go together. That would be incentive for me."

"Where's your gym?" I liked his idea. I'd thought about a gym but always decided it would be a waste of money since I wouldn't know anyone there and so I'd feel uncomfortable and not go after all. But if I joined Jamie's gym, I'd know him. And I'd get to keep seeing him, even if after tonight he decided he just wanted to be friends, whatever tonight ended up being.

He gave me the address. "It's near my place, and you can take the T there too."

"It's Boston–everything's near the T."

He laughed. "Thank god for that. So, what do you do for a living?"

"I'm an accountant."

"So lots of adding and subtracting?"

"The computer does the worst of that."

He laughed again. "I like your sense of humor."

I smiled in reply. I liked numbers, liked making them work. Liked tax returns, even, but I wasn't going to say that to Jamie yet. Maybe later, if he didn't make fun of me for being one of those guys with the big glasses...actually, that was pretty much what I was. "What kind of pizza do you like?"

"My favorite's hamburger and onion, but I'm pretty easy. Anything but anchovies."

I couldn't think of anything to say, with the lights from the store windows we walked by shining on his face and making him look even more like a Greek god.

"Wait, are anchovies your thing?"

He sounded a little worried, and I didn't want that, so I made myself speak. "No, I can take them or leave them. My favorite toppings are hamburger, bacon and onion, although not usually together." I liked pineapple with bacon, but that might seem too weird to him.

He chuckled. "Yeah, that might be a strange combo. Have you ever thought about having bacon and pineapple? It's different, I know, but it's great at Tim's, the place we're going."

Since it was his suggestion... "Sure. Let's have that." I thought about leaving it at that, but what kind of friend would I be if I did? "I've liked that combination before."

He was beaming by the time I finished speaking. "That's great. I had a feeling you'd like that combo." He took my hand in his and squeezed. "Next you'll tell me you like draft pitchers, not bottles."

I laughed. "Good draft, yeah."

"I'll let you pick it out. Then you can't blame me if you don't like it, but I'll get to blame you."

He grinned at me, so I knew he was teasing, and we laughed together as we kept walking, still holding hands. I liked this. I liked how comfortable I felt with him and how fun it was to do something as simple as walk down a street with him. It had been years since I'd been this happy.

I hoped I could be what he wanted. I'd try. I should have read more in the books, but maybe he'd like showing me. I liked that thought.

"Here we are." He turned to go in an open door and tugged me along with him.

The place was bigger than I'd thought from the outside, with long wooden tables running the length of the place and benches to match, a counter in the back with a list of ingredients posted on the wall, as well as the prices for the various sizes of pizzas and combinations, and ovens well behind the counter. I took a deep sniff, and my mouth started watering. Yes, this place made good pizza. I was sure of that.

"I vote for a large bacon and pineapple pizza. How about it?"

The good smells of browning dough and all kinds of toppings were making my stomach rumble. "I vote for a half bacon and pineapple, half hamburger and onion pizza. Large, of course."

"I like a man who likes his pizza. Yeah, let's do that. C'mon." He tugged at my hand, which he was still holding. "Let's order. Know what beer you're going to pick?"

I hadn't seen the beer list yet, but a quick check showed me that it was at the end of the pizza listings. I scanned it. "Harpoon, definitely. The IPA or the Ale, though, hard to choose between them."

"I'd go for the India Pale Ale."

"Nice to know you have good taste in beer."

He let go of my hand and in the same motion slung his arm around my shoulders. "I have good taste in men too."

I stiffened, then made myself relax. Jamie wasn't stupid. If he felt it was safe to put his arm around me here, it probably was.

"Sorry," he said softly. "Didn't think you'd..." He took his arm away and looked away from me. "Sorry."

I hated how sad he sounded. "I'm new to this, Jamie." I tried to speak softly too. "To being in public with a guy–a guy I like and–" I gulped "–I'm on a date with." He turned back toward me, his eyes bright. "I'm sorry. Cut me some slack?"

"Yeah, David, as much as you need. Hey, does anyone call you Davy?"

His voice was happy again, and I was happy too. "Not since I was a kid."

"Mind if I do?"

"No. Go ahead." I liked him wanting to give me a nickname.

"We'll be Davy and Jamie." He headed for the counter to order, and I went with him. "Hey, they almost rhyme. Cool, huh?"

I laughed as we took our place at the end of the short line. "I like that."

"Me too." He grinned. "And I like you."

I was looking into his happy green eyes, and all I wanted to do was be with him. "I like you too."

The line moved, and we were up at the counter. We ordered the pizza and beer, which Jamie insisted on paying for.

"I asked you out. You can buy next time," he said with a grin, and the woman taking the order beamed at us both. I knew I was turning red as I nodded agreement and put my wallet back in my pants pocket, but I'd survive.

He thought that this was a date, the same as I did, and he still was talking about a next time. Wow.

The pizza was really good, and we ate it all, with the beer to wash it down. I found out that he liked to watch sports, especially baseball and soccer, didn't cook much, and read a lot of books.

"Anything that looks good when I'm shelving, I note where it is and pick it up later or read it on my breaks. It's a good system, keeps me out of trouble." He wiped his mouth with a napkin. "Not that I get into trouble much, really. I'm a boring guy."

"No, you're not." There was no way I could believe that.

"Well, thanks." He smiled–I really liked his smile– and shook his head. "Are you done?"

I laughed. "We ate all of it, so yeah."

He laughed too. "Good point. But we could get some more beer if you wanted."

"No, thanks."

"The bar then?"

Right, he was going to take me to the gay bar. I'd been having such a good time with him I'd almost forgotten. I nodded.

He stood. "Let's go. There should be some people there by now."

We cleared the table and headed outside.

"Where's the bar?"

He pointed down the street. "There."

It had a small sign, Peter's Place. I'd have never known it was anything but a regular bar, but if Jamie said it was a gay bar, I believed him, and I'd go there, with him.

I swallowed. Why wasn't this easier? "All right."

Jamie reached out and took my hand. "We don't have to do this tonight. The bar will be there whenever you feel like going."

I'd resolved not to be a coward, and I was not going to back down now. "I want to go."

"I remember the first gay bar I went to. God, was that a disaster." I couldn't imagine him as anything but gorgeous and confident, but I had to believe him, hearing the distant pain in his voice and feeling the tightness of his hold. "That's why I wanted to take you–because it's not easy walking into some place you've never been and only thought about going all by yourself. Plus, what I said before. Even more now."

I couldn't help smiling, remembering him declaring he wanted a chance with me. "Yeah, I like that reason."

"We don't have to stay long." He had an eager look in his eyes.

"No, we don't." I squeezed his hand. "We don't even have to have a drink."

"No, if we go in we'll have to have a drink or we'll get thrown out." He was grinning now. "C'mon. I'll buy."

"You bought dinner." We were walking toward the bar, hand in hand, and I was happy.

"So? I want to. You can buy next time."

Next time. I liked that thought a whole lot, but I wasn't going to back down on this. "Come on. It's my turn."

"I like the thought of taking turns." His voice was husky and low, and I swallowed. He wasn't talking about buying drinks–he was talking about sex. "Sure. You buy."

I swallowed again. God, my cock was hard. Why

the hell were we going somewhere public anyway?

We were at the wooden door. Next we'd go in.

I was very glad Jamie was there with me.

He blew out a breath and reached for the handle with his free hand and pulled the door open. "Ready or not, here we come."

We were both laughing at that when we walked into the bar.

It didn't look any different from any other bar I'd ever been in, with its plain wooden tables, plain wooden chairs, framed beer posters and memorabilia on the walls, and a dark polished wooden bar with a lot of taps for drafts. There were some men at the bar and others at the tables. The place was about half full. There weren't any women there, but that wasn't too unusual either.

A couple of men turned to look at us, and one called to Jamie to come over.

"Not tonight, Carl. Got a date." He looked so proud, and I couldn't help smiling. How had I gotten so lucky?

"Can't take any competition, huh?"

"Sure I can, but why should I?"

"C'mon over, sunshine."

He was talking to me?

"I'll tell you some stories about old Jamie there and show you a better time than he ever could." He patted the back of the chair next to him.

What was with this annoying man? I didn't even know him, and he was trying to ruin my evening. I wasn't going to let him do that.

"No, thanks." I looked away from the man, who was laughing, and at Jamie, who was definitely not laughing. He was giving the guy a hard stare. "Jamie." He blinked and looked at me. "Ignore him. I'm going to, since I'm with the best-looking guy here." I made sure to say that loud enough for this Carl to hear.

Jamie blinked again, then grinned. "You got that wrong. *I'm* with the best looking guy here."

He squeezed my hand, and I squeezed his. I wanted

to argue with that, since I knew I wasn't good-looking, but he sounded so happy and sure that I didn't. "Thanks."

"Sure. Sit down, and I'll get us some beers. 'Kay?"

Carl had stopped looking at us, and all the other men were minding their own business.

"I told you I was buying."

Jamie held out his hand. "So give me some money." I dug into my pocket for my wallet. "What kind do you want?"

"Just some soda." I didn't need any more to drink. I was with him, in a gay bar.

He blinked, then nodded. "Yeah, I don't need any more alcohol either." He grinned. "But it'll be pricey soda."

Why would I care about that? I handed him a ten and took his jacket from him. "I'll take a Coke, please."

"Coming up."

He headed toward the bar. I went to an empty table away from the other people, putting Jamie's jacket on the back of one chair and my bag on the floor by the one across from it, sat in the second chair, and took some deep breaths. Being in a gay bar with Jamie was heady stuff.

Jamie was already heading back to me, which made me smile. I wanted to be with him, not by myself. I was by myself too much of the time.

He set two glasses on the table, each with a straw topped with the end of the white wrapping. "Two pricey sodas, as you ordered. I'll give you the change later, if that's okay."

"Thanks. That's fine." I reached for one of the glasses and plucked off the wrapping, then raised my glass. "To us."

Jamie's smile was wide and happy. "Yeah, to us."

We both drank, then Jamie set his glass on the table. "Hey, about when we came in."

"Yes?" What was the problem?

"Sorry about that. I can be a dick sometimes.

Didn't mean to let you see it this soon, though."

I leaned toward him. I didn't know where this confidence was coming from, but hell, I'd take it. "Did you say I could see your dick?"

His eyes widened. "Now?" He reached down, with a mischievous look in his eyes. "Sure, but we'll get thrown out."

"Not now." We were both laughing. "God, I don't believe I said that."

"I love that you said that. And yeah, I'll show you my dick later, if you show me yours."

Oh yes. I nodded.

He put his hand on my arm. "Good."

We had to change the subject now, or I'd drag him out of there. I cleared my throat. "Do you like your job?"

He let go of my arm and leaned back in his chair. "Most days. Today a lot."

"Why today?"

He laughed softly. "Cause you walked in, David. I thought that would have been obvious."

I swallowed. "I'm not good at flirting, Jamie."

"I'm not flirting."

I believed him. "Okay. Thanks."

We were both quiet after that, but it was a good quiet. We sat and drank our Cokes and looked at each other. I liked it.

Jamie came back from the bathroom–I'd gone a few minutes before, courtesy of the beers with dinner–sat back down, drank the last of his Coke, and put down the glass. "That was good."

I finished the last of mine. "Yeah, it was."

"So, got any questions about those books?" He was smiling one of the warmest smiles I'd ever seen. "Anything at all?"

I smiled too. "Not really."

"They're good books."

"They seem to be." It took me a moment to get up

the courage to say what I wanted to. We were in a gay bar. We could talk about gay things there. "I do have a list I'd like you to look at, though. It's my list of things I want to try." And with him if at all possible, which I hoped he'd understand without me saying so. I dug the list out of my pocket and smoothed it out on the table, then handed it to him.

He scanned it, then looked at me. "I like your list."

"We can't do anything about it here, though," I said softly, tapping into courage I hadn't known I had. "But we could somewhere else. Like my place, or yours." I hoped he'd want to take me to his place. He'd said earlier that he wanted me in his bed, and that sounded great to me.

"Oh yeah." He had an intense look in his eyes. "At my place. I want you there."

My heart was pounding. "I want to be there." And I didn't want to be at this bar any longer. I'd found who I wanted, and I wasn't going to wait any longer to be alone with him. "Let's go."

He was up and out of his chair before I finished. "Yeah. Let's go." He grabbed his jacket.

I grabbed my bag and the list as I stood. "Is your place far from here?"

"A few T stops. Come on. I don't want to wait."

Neither did I. "Yes."

He wasn't smiling, but I liked the look on his face anyway. I'd put it there. Maybe that was why I liked it.

He took my hand when we were outside. "I'm glad you're coming home with me, Davy." His voice was low. "I really am."

"I'm glad you want me to come home with you."

He squeezed my hand. "I'm smarter than I look."

I couldn't help smiling at that as we started walking. "You look pretty smart."

"Yeah?" He grinned at me. "That's not what I hear."

"Then what you hear is wrong."

He laughed but didn't say anything more.

I looked around and saw the entrance to a T stop ahead and across the street, so I veered toward it.

He pulled me back before I could step off the curb. "Hey! This is Boston! Don't cross without looking."

I blinked at him. "I looked."

"Oh." He blinked too. "I...sorry."

I couldn't help smiling. I liked that he cared. "No prob."

I made sure he saw me look both ways before I pulled at his hand to cross the street, and this time, he didn't stop me.

When we were inside his small, neat living room, he dropped his jacket on a nearby chair, and I put down my bag.

"It's up to you what we do now, Davy."

He was facing me, waiting for me to say or do something, looking even more gorgeous than when I'd first seen him, and I realized yes, I could do what I wanted–kiss him.

So I did.

"Wow," he breathed when we broke for air and for me to take off my glasses. "Why did we waste all that time out?"

I wanted to laugh, but I was still panting. "We had to get to know each other."

"Yeah. We did." He angled his head. "I want to kiss you all night."

That sounded good to me. I nodded and kissed him again.

When we broke the next time, my cheeks felt a little scraped from his stubble, but I didn't care about that, not with his hands pulling my shirt out of my pants. I'd already pulled his up and had my hands on his bare, warm skin.

"Wanna sit down?"

I glanced at his couch. It looked comfortable enough, and I wasn't sure I wanted to go into his bedroom quite yet. "Any chance of anyone walking in on us?"

His hands started tracing patterns on my skin, and I found myself breathing even harder. "No, so whatever you want to do, wherever you want to do it, we're good."

I tried to think about what items on my list would be reasonable to try next, but I couldn't think too well, so I just did what I wanted to do, which was to touch his back and kiss his neck.

He moaned, then took a deep breath and pulled me over to the couch and down on it. "That's better."

And he started kissing me again.

The next time we broke, both of our shirts and undershirts were off, and I'd learned that I liked having my nipples stroked just about as much as Jamie did.

"I really want you in my bed." Jamie's voice was hoarse. "Please."

That sounded great to me. I nodded and tried to stand, which didn't go too well, but after a moment I got the hang of it. Jamie took my hand and headed out of the room, went by one door–"The bathroom," he pointed out–then opened another door. "My room."

I looked around the room. Another small room, but with a big bed in it.

Oh.

He was inside already. "C'mon in, Davy." He sat down on the bed and patted the dark blue blanket next to him. "It's nice and comfortable."

I walked over to him, and he smiled up at me. I did like his smile. "You have a nice room."

"Nicer with you in it."

"Thanks." I sat down next to him and decided I wanted to make the next move. "Want to kiss some more?"

His smile turned into a happy grin. "Oh yeah." He turned his body to face me and started kissing me again.

It didn't take long for us to end up stretched out on the bed, rubbing against each other, touching each other, and yeah, kissing like we were never going to stop.

This was more than I'd ever thought I'd get, and I loved it. But was it enough for Jamie?

I broke away from him and rolled over onto my back. "Jamie?" It was hard to talk, but I had to try.

"Yeah?" He looked at me with dazed eyes. "Something wrong?"

"No. Are you...do you like this?"

He smiled. "Davy, I *love* this. We can do this all night, nothing more, and I will be the happiest guy in the whole damned city, I promise you."

"I like this too. But I thought maybe you'd want more."

"It's your first time, right?" I nodded. "Worry about what *you* want, not what I want. I have what I want."

He sounded so sure that I had to believe him, and I decided I would do what I wanted, and now. "All right." I reached down to my pants. "I want to be naked with you."

His eyes widened. "Wow. Yeah. Oh yeah."

"I want you naked too." I lifted my hips and pulled off my pants and dropped them on the floor.

He grinned and undid his belt. "You got it, Davy."

"Not yet I don't."

He pulled his jeans off. "Now you do."

His body was gorgeous. I hoped he liked how I looked, but I thought probably so since his cock was standing up, just like mine, but not like mine. I reached over to touch it–velvety, hot, perfect–and he moaned. I looked up at him. Yes, he liked this. So I wrapped my hand around his cock and squeezed and got another moan out of him.

"Can I touch you?" His voice was hoarse, and his muscles were tensed. "God, Davy."

I was really hard, and I liked the thought of him touching and stroking me. "Yes." Then I gasped as his warm fingers circled my cock.

This was so, so much better than touching myself.

It was like flying. I closed my eyes and arched my back. Was I going to come just from this?

"Yeah," I heard Jamie breathe. He kept working me. How did he know just what I liked? "God, yeah."

Then I cried out and shot.

Now it was over. Dammit.

I felt a kiss on my cheek and Jamie's warm body pressing against mine. "Thanks."

Why the hell was he thanking me? I opened my eyes to find that he was smiling.

"Sorry. I'm not usually that quick, but you got me so hot..." He shrugged, still smiling. "Hell, I've been on the edge of coming just about all night. I guess I'm lucky I lasted this long. Promise next time I'll last longer, unless you like me this way."

I realized my hand was sticky. He'd come too, then. I'd made him come.

I smiled. "I like you any way."

"Great." He reached over and grabbed some tissues and handed them to me, then got some for himself. "I hate to say this, but I have to get some sleep."

I tensed. Was he going to ask me to leave?

He tossed his tissues into a wastebasket by the door. "You ready to sleep too?"

He wanted me to stay. "Yes, you wore me out." I smiled at him.

He laughed. "I like that."

"And I wore you out."

"Yeah, you did." He pulled down the covers on his side, pushed the blanket to the end of the bed, and pulled the sheet over himself. "I can set the alarm for you if you like."

The cool sheets felt good against my skin. "No, thanks. I'll wake up when the sun comes in." And it would, since there were no blinds or curtains on the window. Not that I minded.

He laughed softly. "I won't, so make sure you wake me, okay? I was hoping we could shower together, and I want to buy you breakfast."

"I'd like that." It wouldn't matter if I came in a little late. People came in a little late all the time and just worked through lunch or stayed later.

He smiled at me. "We'll get to the rest of your list next time."

"Yes. Fine." I turned over, smiled into the pillow as his arm came around my chest and pulled me against him, and closed my eyes.

We really would have a next time. I had found my courage, and I was so glad.

The End

Fast Forward

The fog was rolling over Twin Peaks as it often did on summer nights in San Francisco. It crept up over the city's hills and through its valleys. Gabe loved the way it blanketed the city each night. It obscured views and provided a sense of nocturnal anonymity for the city's residents. He also loved the way the fog began its daily, ritualistic disappearing act in the mornings.

Gabe had seen his share of debauchery in San Francisco. He'd moved to the city right after college and had been there ever since. At 33, he felt like he had "been there, done that" one too many times. With each guy he hooked up with, the city seemed to grow smaller and close in on him.

Gabe had grown up and gone to college in Los Angeles, so San Francisco always seemed small in comparison. Initially, the small-town feeling of a so-called big city was attractive. Occasionally he longed for a bigger, better, faster city lifestyle. And that's not what San Francisco had to offer. The dot-com boom was what primarily lured Gabe with its promise of big money and get-rich-quick tech jobs. He managed to eke out a pretty good living for a couple of years. He'd saved a ton of money and spent much, much more. There was no end to the boys, booze, and parties during those years.

Gabe had no trouble finding hot guys to date or fuck around with. One ex-boyfriend often referred to him as the "boy-next-door" type. He was six feet tall with thick brown hair and piercing blue eyes. His cheeks possessed two irresistible dimples when he smiled. He knew that he could pretty much seal any deal with one coy, dimpled smirk. He worked out regularly to keep his body hard and fit. His nicely sculpted pecs gave way to tight abs that were accompanied by bulging biceps, and a bubble butt that looked great in his low-rise jeans. Not to mention the feature gay guys cared about most–his thick eight-inch member. While Gabe entertained the notion of being versatile, it was hard not to love topping a stud when you had an endowment like his.

To say that Gabe had bad luck with relationships was an understatement. It seemed he had a propensity for meeting the man of his dreams, only to discover that each one was more like the man of his nightmares. Like, for example, the ex-boyfriend who was Ivy League-educated and an investment banker by day, and then, as Gabe discovered too late, a high-priced hooker by night. Or the ex-boyfriend who seemed so kind and gentle, but couldn't bring himself to make a single decision without calling his mother to ask her opinion first. Unearthing hidden neuroses seemed to be Gabe's special talent; it was one that he wasn't particularly proud of. After a number of these Mr. Not-so-perfect boyfriends, Gabe started hoping he'd already dated all the crazies and would fall in love with a sane one.

It certainly didn't help that Gabe was burning the candle at both ends during those years. He woke up early to hit the gym every morning. Then it was off to work for hours of ceaseless tech work. He'd stop off to have drinks with friends after work each night, bounce from bar to bar with friends until the wee hours of the morning, and then stumble home in a boozy daze. With so much time spent in the "scene," Gabe didn't spend much time reflecting on himself or his love life.

Then the dot-com bubble burst. The corporate money dried up, and so did the nightlife. Boys moved away and jobs disappeared. Although Gabe had partied hard, he'd worked even harder and built himself a nice cushion. When the company he worked for closed its doors, he decided to slow down and enjoy life in a somewhat different way.

After selling his expensive car and moving to a more reasonably priced apartment in the Castro, Gabe then made the biggest lifestyle change of all. He decided to get a job as a clerk at Rainbow Video, the local gay video store known more for its massive porn collection than for its more traditional movies. He figured it would be a good way to settle down, get to know his neighbors, and most importantly, have access to free gay porn. As if swept away by the fog overnight, his old life and the city lifestyle that had encouraged it were gone.

Gabe liked the change of pace working at the video store. He worked eight hours from 2pm to 10pm every day except Sundays and Mondays. It paid just enough to cover rent and his minimal bills. Thanks to his sizeable savings, he could still treat himself and a date to the occasional fancy dinner, or go out for drinks with friends once a week or so.

In the midst of all these changes, Gabe also decided to slow down his search for a boyfriend. Given his shitty track record with guys, he decided to take a break from long-term relationships, and just enjoy occasional one-night stands and regular sex with a few fuck buddies. While the sex was plentiful, obligation-free, and pretty often amazing, he still held out hope that one of his random hookups might miraculously end up being Mr. Right instead of just Mr. Right Now.

Gabe enjoyed the feeling of being more centered and grounded. When he went out with friends, it felt more genuine. He cared what his friends had to say and what they were going through. And likewise, his friends seemed interested in learning more about what made Gabe tick. All of this positivity was, in no small part, due to the lack of booze and party lifestyle. Gabe was growing up and, on many levels, his lifestyle change was responsible.

One of the new friendships he developed not long

after moving into his new home turned out to be one of the most comfortable he'd ever had in his life. By slowing down and not focusing solely on work and his rocky relationships with guys, Gabe started taking notice of the other fascinating people in his life. One evening as he came home to his new apartment in the Castro, he passed a vibrantly redheaded woman leaving his apartment building. She was short and had a naturally curvy figure. Tethered to her wrist was a small fluffy dog prancing in anticipation of its nightly walk.

Gabe held the door open for his neighbor. She looked up, and said, "Thanks. You must be the new neighbor. My name is Alara and I live in 2B."

"Hi! Nice to meet you," said Gabe. "I moved into 3A a couple of weeks ago. And who is this pretty princess?"

"I already told you my name is Alara," she quipped.

Gabe and Alara both giggled at the joke. "This is my sweet Trixie. She's pleased to meet you."

Gabe stooped down and Trixie trotted over to say hello. He offered his hand, and Trixie sniffed it. Then she wiggled her body and sneezed on his hand. Gabe had always liked animals and didn't mind the sneeze. Gabe wiped his hand on his jeans and patted Trixie's head with his dry hand.

"She likes you. You know, she doesn't like everyone. She only sneezes on boys she really *really* likes," explained Alara. "I guess that means you're good people. If you ever need to borrow the proverbial cup of sugar, you know where to find me. In fact, if you'd like to come over for tea sometime, just give a knock at the door. Trixie and I like cute, gay company." Alara winked as she offered the compliment. Gabe blushed.

"Thanks, I'll take you up on that offer. I'm doing this whole 'slow down and smell the roses' sorta thing. So, a tea date sounds right up my alley. Have a nice walk and I'll see you soon," Gabe said as he shut the door behind Alara and Trixie. Gabe felt an immediate and strong connection to her. Although it had been years since he'd had a close female friend, Gabe knew that Alara was going to be someone he could open up to.

A typical day at the Rainbow Video was fairly uneventful. And Gabe liked it that way. The store was already open by the time he showed up for his shift at 2 that afternoon. Usually it was pretty quiet until 4. That's when guys started getting off work and stopping by to pick up their nightly wank material. Most of the guys were Castro regulars and Gabe learned their names quickly. He always found it interesting to see which guys rented which type of porn. Without fail, it was always the quiet, demure types that rented the most intense types of porn. This didn't surprise Gabe. Like they said, the shy ones often had the kinkiest sex lives.

Gabe also started to take videos home with him when he closed up shop each night–it was easier than looking for sex each night. And, there was no worry of complicated relationship stuff developing between him and a video. He tried not to date any of the regulars, but sometimes the hot studs knew just the right things to say to pique his interest. Still, though, he kept it casual and didn't sleep with anyone more than once.

One Friday afternoon Gabe was sitting behind the counter as usual when the door buzzer sounded. Gabe looked up to see which regular customer was coming to rent some porn. But what Gabe saw wasn't one of the regulars at all. Instead, Gabe laid eyes on the sexiest young specimen of man-flesh that he'd seen in years. Gabe made a mental note about how happy he was to be behind the counter, because his cock had sprung to full attention.

Gabe couldn't take his eyes off of this new kid. He was about 5'9", blond, and had big dazzling green eyes. He had a nice physique with broad shoulders and a tiny waist. Gabe imagined that the kid probably had played high school football or wrestled. As Gabe's eyes roved downward they got stuck on the new guy's most notable feature: his bubble butt.

"Man, I sure would love to get my hands on that ass..." Gabe murmured under his breath.

Gabe studied the blondie's actions with fascination. He noted how the kid seemed to dilly-dally in the non-porn section, and edged ever closer to the porn aisles.

"How cute. He's too nervous to just go look at the porn," Gabe thought to himself.

Finally the newbie picked up *The Bourne Supremacy* and headed toward Gabe at the check out counter.

"Hey there, a Matt Damon fan, huh?" Gabe queried.

"Heh, yeah I guess so," the kid said. "I missed it when it was in the theater, so I figured I'd watch it now. This is my first time here, so do I need to open an account?"

"Yep! Let me get the paperwork and explain our rental policy."

Gabe explained the various rental plans and rates and asked for the kid's ID. "So, Thomas, you're from Cleveland, huh?" Gabe asked as he studied the Ohio driver's license.

"Well, actually it's Tom, er, Tommy. I mean, well...um...people call me Tom but my friends call me Tommy. Call me Tommy," he said as he blushed and looked down at the counter.

Gabe found it endearing that Tommy was so shy and nervous in response to the slightest bit of flirtation.

"Okay. Tommy it is. I'm Gabe. What brings you to San Fran?" Gabe flirted some more.

"I grew up in Cleveland and went to Notre Dame for college. I just graduated and moved here a few weeks ago. I start a new job at Levi Strauss as an accountant next week," Tommy explained.

Gabe stared, mesmerized, into Tommy's eyes as the kid spoke. He couldn't help but think that the vibrant green eyes betrayed an innocence and awe at the big gay city.

Gabe took down Tommy's new address in San Francisco and noted that it was only five or six blocks from his own house. After entering all the information into the store's computer and scanning the video, Tommy's rental was complete.

"Well, that's about it. Hope you enjoy watching Matt Damon get all sweaty doing spy stuff," said Gabe, slightly disappointed that their interaction was nearing its end.

"Thanks, I'll try."

"And, good luck with your first day of work next week. Hope to see you again real soon," Gabe said as he winked and unleashed his dimpled smile.

Tommy grinned from ear to ear and blushed bright red. "Yeah, see you soon, I hope."

Gabe watched as the most tempting ass he'd ever seen moved away toward the door. Under the counter his cock was hard and aching for release. It was still early and no one else was in the store. So, Gabe put up the "back in 10 minutes" sign in the doorway, locked the door, and headed for the staff bathroom.

Once he was in the privacy of the bathroom, Gabe released his rock-hard dick from his pants, spat in his hand, and started stroking wildly. He closed his eyes and relived the flirtatious interaction he'd just had with Tommy. Within a minute or two an electric pulse sent shivers down his spine and his abs contracted. His dick spasmed and he shot rope after rope of white, thick come into the toilet bowl. He wiped the last bit of come off of the sensitive tip of his cock, washed his hands, and headed back to open up the store again.

Sitting at the counter in post-orgasmic bliss, Gabe couldn't stop thinking about Tommy. He wanted this kid in a bad way. But it was more than that, too. It was *more* than sexual. Then it hit him: he was crushing on Tommy, and crushing hard.

A few nights later Gabe saw Alara in the lobby again. They were both headed upstairs and she offered him some tea. Gabe gladly accepted, and after dropping off his things in his apartment, stopped over at 2B. Alara's apartment was warm and inviting, and tastefully decorated with African art. She guided Gabe to the couch and headed into the kitchen to prepare the tea.

Just as he sat down, Trixie trotted up and jumped up into his lap. He started to pet the top of her head. Suddenly her body gave a now familiar wiggle and she sneezed into Gabe's lap. Alara entered with the tea, shaking her head in amusement at her little dog's display of affection.

As they sat and chatted, Gabe learned that Alara had spent many years in Africa, helping to build schools and teaching children how to read. While they sipped their tea, she regaled him with incredible stories of her African adventures. Then, ever the gracious hostess, Alara prompted Gabe to tell her about himself. Gabe described why he'd come to San Francisco, explained the boozy years, the fast-paced work life, his deliberate lifestyle change, his swearing off relationships, and of course, his disastrous taste in men.

Gabe was comforted that Alara had almost as many, if not more, bad relationship stories to share. They commiserated and bonded over their boyfriends' shared psychoses. And even though he hadn't been able to get Tommy out of his head since their encounter, Gabe had forgotten to mention it to Alara.

"So, I did sorta meet this guy at the store the other day. I know I promised myself I wasn't going to get back into a relationship anytime soon. But, this guy is so cute, and smart, and has the hottest little butt. And I just can't stop thinking about him. He even has me rethinking my moratorium on relationships," Gabe confessed to Alara.

"Oooh, a crush! This sounds juicy," said Alara as she sat forward. "Talk."

Gabe recounted his exchange with Tommy nearly word for word.

"After he left, I was so turned on, I had to go take

some...private time...in the staff bathroom." Gabe wasn't sure if this was over-sharing, but Alara didn't seem to bat an eyelash at the steamy revelation.

"That sounds fun. Do you think you're going to ask him out?"

"I don't know," Gabe wondered aloud. "He sure seems like my type. He's just so new to the city. Maybe I should give him a few weeks to get used to it here before I make a move."

"Follow your instincts," Alara advised. "And keep me posted with all the spicy details when you finally take things to the next level."

Gabe promised her that she would be the first to know if anything new happened with Tommy. And, since it was getting late, they finished their tea and he headed upstairs to his apartment. He went straight to bed and fell fast asleep with thoughts of Tommy on his mind.

Somewhere in the middle of the night, Gabe dreamt vividly of Tommy. In his dream world, Tommy's appearance in Gabe's bedroom doorway made total sense. Tommy stood there with his shirt off, one arm pressed against the doorframe. His muscular chest and six-pack abs shone beautifully in the moonlight that spilled in through the bedroom window.

The short blond stud sauntered over to Gabe's bed. Gabe looked up and the two stared at each other. The truth was there, barely concealed behind their eyes. They wanted each other, badly. Tommy fell to the bed and they embraced. Gabe could feel the kid's heart pounding in his chest and smell his sweet scent.

Suddenly they were kissing passionately. Their tongues flicked around and explored each other. Tommy sucked on Gabe's tongue–something that made Gabe go wild with passion. Gabe lost himself for what seemed like an eternity in this intense and intimate connection. A wet spot was seeping through the sheet where Gabe's cock was begging for attention.

As if Tommy could read his mind, he pulled back

the light cotton sheet exposing Gabe's beautiful cock to the moonlit room. Tommy licked his way down Gabe's chest, down further past his abs, finally reaching his destination. Without using his hands, Tommy enveloped Gabe's cock with his lips. Gabe could feel Tommy's tongue gently massaging his cock, as his lips moved up and down the thick shaft.

Gabe was rock hard, and he was sure his dick was bigger and harder than he'd ever known it to be. Somewhere a glimmer of reality seeped in and he knew this was because in his dream world anything was possible, especially his dick growing by several inches.

While Tommy continued to orally fixate on Gabe's member, Gabe let his fingers explore Tommy's body. They crawled and danced all over the kid's thick, powerful muscles, tracing each peak and valley. Gabe pulled Tommy's ass toward him. Tommy expertly repositioned himself so that his ass was in the air near Gabe's face, all the while never ceasing his rhythm and suction on Gabe's dick. Gabe had unfettered access to Tommy's ass. He dove in and began breathing heavily on the kid's pink hole. Gabe extended his tongue and licked up from Tommy's balls, up into his smooth ass crack. Tommy shuddered and Gabe felt a marked change in the pace of the stud's oral treatment of his cock. This attention to his ass was driving him wild.

Gabe continued to tease and flick his tongue across Tommy's ass. Gabe gently applied pressure with his forefinger, and felt Tommy's hole quiver and tighten. With one hand, Gabe stroked Tommy's dick while his finger continued its forward movement. Slowly Gabe's fingertip slid past Tommy's sphincter. Tommy released Gabe's dick from his mouth, arched his back, and gasped. Gabe kissed the spot where his digit was buried, and then kissed and playfully nibbled at Tommy's muscled ass cheeks. Gabe felt Tommy relax all over, as the kid returned to work on Gabe's dick. His finger slid even further in, until it was buried to the first knuckle. He worked his finger carefully back and forth.   Tommy's hips started to buck and drive backward, engulfing the rest of Gabe's finger.

Without warning, and at a lighting speed possible only in a dream, Tommy lifted his head and swung around to face Gabe. Staring into Tommy's eyes, Gabe couldn't help but be mesmerized by the Adonis-like features of the blond stud above him. He gazed deeply into Tommy's green eyes, and wanted everything about him: mind, body, and soul. Their lips met again, and their tongues darted into each other's mouths. Lost in the intensity, Gabe barely noticed Tommy's hand reach back and grasp Gabe's cock. It wasn't until Gabe felt Tommy's willing rosebud press down on the tip of his cock that he realized he was about to penetrate and become one with the object of his desire.

Tommy lowered himself down, stopping just after Gabe's thick mushroom tip slipped in. Gabe wanted more, he wanted to be buried in Tommy's promised land, to feel warm, and connected, and one with this amazing man on top of him. He thrust his hips up, sliding his dick half way into Tommy's butt. The friction and heat surrounding his dick were electrifying as Gabe pulled out slightly and thrust upward again. Tommy's eyes rolled back into his head and he moaned as Gabe reached near full penetration.

Suddenly, Tommy opened his eyes, arched his back and started to rock back and forth. Gabe reached up and grasped Tommy's beautiful cock in his hand. Each time Tommy lowered himself fully onto Gabe's dick and Gabe felt himself bottom out inside of Tommy, he also felt Tommy's dick pulsate in his hand. "This kid definitely loves having a dick in his ass," thought Gabe.

Then Tommy brought his legs up next to Gabe's hips, and started to use his massive quads to lift and lower himself onto Gabe's engorged member. He pulled nearly all the way out before slamming his full weight back down into Gabe's groin. Each time Tommy would slam his ass down, he'd then pull back up, tightening his ass around Gabe's cock on his ascent.

Gabe was lost in intense pleasure. Tommy was riding him like no other bottom ever had. Gabe got lost in the sensations and visual stimulation of watching his massive cock disappear and then reappear with Tommy's each muscular movement.

Suddenly, without warning, Tommy's dick surged and pulsed. Gabe too, was close to the brink. Then as Gabe felt Tommy's hot seed cover his own chest, he felt an intense and unfathomable orgasm begin deep in his groin and erupt upward. The warm intensity of Gabe's orgasm lasted for what seemed like a lifetime. He lay there in the bed, dizzily awash in sexual bliss. He looked up and saw that Tommy was there, but fading. Gabe could feel Tommy's weight dissipating, as Tommy became more of a shadow. Gabe could see clean through the hologram-like impression of his crush now. The last thing Gabe remembered was the impish grin on Tommy's face before he disappeared without a trace.

Gabe's eyes snapped open. He immediately squinted at the morning sunlight that had now filled the room. He looked around, noting that his room looked exactly how he'd left it when he'd gone to bed the night before. As his head cleared, he still vividly remembered the intense sexual connection he'd had with Tommy during the night. He pulled back his sheets, revealing the result of his nocturnal adventure. His groin and chest were covered with his cold, half-dried ejaculate and his sheets were a wet sticky mess. He couldn't wipe the grin from his face as he stumbled into the bathroom and eventually felt the warm water begin to wash away the evidence of his unconscious sexual encounter with Tommy.

Only a few days later, Tommy came by the video store again. Unfortunately, it was after 5, and therefore "rush hour" at the video shop. As Tommy made his way to the counter with yet another non-X-rated video, Gabe realized there wouldn't be time to flirt. There were several other guys in line behind Tommy, all eagerly waiting to rent their porn so they could go home and jack off.

"Hey there. Good to see you again," said Gabe as Tommy approached the counter. A broad smile spread across Gabe's face as he remembered his dream.

"Good to see you too."

"How's the new job treating you?" asked Gabe, trying to show some interest in the small amount of time he had.

"Oh, it's good. Keeping me pretty busy. This is the first time I've been able to watch a movie since work started," confessed Tommy.

The transaction complete, Gabe said, "Well, don't be a stranger and don't work too hard."

"I'll try," Tommy responded with a grin. "See ya."

Over the next several weeks Gabe and Tommy had dozens of similar interactions. Tommy always showed up in the store when it was too busy for Gabe to properly flirt with him. And, because Gabe was pretty sure that Alara wouldn't want to hear about his wet dreams, the dream sex he'd had with Tommy was still Gabe's little secret.

Gabe was closing up one night and was disappointed that he hadn't seen Tommy come in to return the video he'd rented the night before. His last chore of the night was to sort through the DVDs that had been returned in the drop box. As he was checking them into the computer system, he noticed Tommy's account pop up as he scanned the movie Tommy had rented. Gabe opened the DVD jewel case to verify that the DVD was inside, as he did with every DVD. But there inside the jewel case staring back at Gabe was a something other than the store's movie. Instead, Gabe saw a blank DVD sitting on top of the store's movie.

Gabe raised his eyebrows in curiosity. "What's this?" he said out loud to the empty store.

He stashed the DVD in his backpack, figuring he'd return it to Tommy when he next saw him. After finishing the rest of his closing tasks, Gabe headed out in the foggy night and trekked home. He reheated some leftovers and was watching some TV as he ate. Then he remembered the DVD in his backpack. An intense desire to know what was on it invaded him. He retrieved his backpack and located the blank DVD. As he held it in his hand he deliberated whether he should watch. Was that invading Tommy's privacy? Would Tommy ever know? Ultimately his curiosity was too strong, and he popped the DVD into his laptop.

For a minute, Gabe thought the blank DVD was just that: blank. He skipped forward through empty footage until something appeared on his screen. It was clearly a person, though badly out of focus. Maybe the person was just way too close to the camera lens. The quality was grainy–clearly shot in low light with a digital camera. There were some rustling noises and then the person moved back from the camera. At first the guy's bare chest came into view. As he moved further back, the camera showed his naked, semi-hard dick. Finally, the guy's face came into view and it was exactly what Gabe was hoping for and yet hoping against too. It was Tommy!

Gabe didn't know what to think, and pushed pause. Should he keep watching? This was clearly Tommy's home video, and who knew what was coming next. Did Tommy accidentally put his home movie in the wrong jewel case? Or...or did he leave it for Gabe on purpose? Was he just too embarrassed to hand it to Gabe personally? That would maybe explain why Tommy had used the drop box for the first time that night.

Gabe's decided to suppress his conscience and pushed play again. Tommy's face and body were in full view. The look on Tommy's face was one Gabe had not seen before. The youthful innocence was still there, but his face betrayed something else too–something slightly sinister. The look was that of a kid daring to get caught with his hand in the cookie jar.

Tommy stood there flexing his cute, muscled body. First he flexed his biceps. He even did the silly thing that all self-obsessed college boys do when flexing in front of a mirror, and kissed his own bulging bicep. Normally Gabe would find this annoying and cocky. But because it was cute, wholesome Tommy doing it, Gabe found it slightly endearing.

Gabe reached down, unzipped his zipper, and pulled out his aroused member. Without taking his eyes off the computer screen, he spit into his hand and began to stroke his dick rhythmically. Tommy continued to flex his muscles, contracting his abs, showing off his triceps and quad. When Tommy turned around to flex his back muscles and to show off his butt, Gabe's cock pulsed hard. Damn, Gabe wanted to grab that cute booty. "I wouldn't just grab it, either." Gabe thought. There were lots of things he could think to do with such a juicy ass.

Tommy turned back around to face the camera. He grabbed a bottle of baby oil and squirted out a small amount into his hand. With his lubed hand, he began to stroke his semi-soft member. After a few strokes, he was rock hard and his dick had turned a bright shade of reddish-purple. Gabe was transfixed and ready to shoot his own load any moment. And he nearly did shoot when on screen, Tommy turned sideways. Suddenly Gabe could see a profile of Tommy's cute butt as he masturbated. Gabe heard Tommy's breathing quicken on screen. Tommy's abs contracted and he hunched slightly forward. His dick then erupted in white-hot jets and his ass muscles contracted tightly. Watching his crush shudder and unload on screen was too much for Gabe, and he too let loose. His spunk shot all over the floor. "Thank god I have wood floors," Gabe mused to himself.

Gabe paused the video and cleaned up his mess. Once the tissues were safely stored in the trash can, Gabe came back to his laptop. He noticed that there were only a few seconds left on the video. "I've watched this far; why stop now?" he thought. He pressed play and watched as Tommy wiped his sticky hand on a towel that had been sitting nearby. Tommy then approached the video camera with an outstretched hand to turn it off. Gabe stared into the camera, and for a few seconds Tommy stared directly back; their gazes locked across the digital divide. Gabe felt as if he could reach out and touch him. It was so real, so intense, so intimate. Then the screen went black, and the spell was broken.

Gabe ejected the DVD from his laptop and put it back into his backpack. He checked the time; it was still early enough in the night. He washed his hands, straightened himself up, and walked downstairs to Alara's apartment. He knocked lightly so we wouldn't disturb her, just in case she was asleep early. A few moments later Alara opened the door. A big, warm smile spread across her face when she saw it was Gabe.

"Hi cutie, how are you?"

"Um, remember when you said you wanted to know if anything new developed with Tommy. Well..."

"Come right on in. Tell me everything," she said as she grabbed his elbow and led him to the couch where Trixie was curled up in a fluffy ball sleeping.

Gabe told her everything. About the weeks of not getting to flirt with Tommy properly. About not seeing him that night when Tommy returned his movie. And about the video. He spared no detail. Gabe even told her about jacking off to the video, although he kept that fairly direct and to the point.

"So, I guess the question is whether he left it for you on purpose or whether it was a mistake," Alara summarized. "What do you think?"

Gabe just shook his head and stared off into the distance. Finally he mumbled, "I wish I knew. This is just so weird and complicated. Nothing even remotely like that has ever happened to me before."

"Well, I guess you could ask him about it when he comes in. Are you going to give him his DVD back next time you see him?"

"If I do give it back, and he doesn't even know he put it in there, that could embarrass him. I know I would be embarrassed. But if he did mean for me to see it, and I don't mention it, then maybe he'll think I'm freaked out. Fuck if I know. I feel like I'm damned if I do, damned if I don't."

"Sweetie, why don't you just take the DVD with you to work and just do what feels right in the moment. Try to read his body language and see what happens," offered Alara.

They agreed that that was the best thing to do. Gabe left Alara's apartment that night feeling a little better than before, but also still awkward and unsure of what to do.

Gabe checked the computer every day for activity on Tommy's account. Several weeks went by and nothing, nada, zilch. Gabe was ready to write off the whole bizarre experience and try to forget it ever happened. That is, until one morning Gabe noticed Tommy had been in to rent a movie the previous day, which had been Gabe's day off. Gabe waited all day anticipating what he would do when Tommy walked through the door. But Tommy never came. Gabe felt deflated. Was Tommy avoiding him? He might never know. Then, just like before, he saw Tommy's rental in the drop box at the end of his shift. Gabe was too nervous to open the case and discover what was inside. Finally, with a deep breath, he cracked open the case. And, sure enough, there was another blank DVD sitting on top of the store's movie.

Gabe was too giddy to wait for home. The store was already closed, so he went into the back room and pulled out his laptop from his backpack. He popped in the DVD. The video indicated that it was only a minute and a half long. Gabe had his dick out in his hand, stroking it as he pressed play. This time there was no blank footage upfront. The video came to life immediately and Gabe was amazed. There in front of him was Tommy's face buried in another man's crotch. Tommy was sucking on a fairly large penis. Although,

Gabe made a mental note, it was not as big as his own. Tommy was anything but apprehensive about having a dick in his mouth. He bobbed, slurped, and simultaneously jacked the anonymous man's member with intensity. Gabe could hear the object of Tommy's attention moan and grunt from above. His hand just barely showed on screen, as he pushed Tommy's head down onto his dick. Gabe was glued to the screen and his cock was close to busting his nut. Just as the video approached the last few seconds, the anonymous man pulled his dick out of Tommy's mouth and shot rope of come onto Tommy's face. The screen went black just as Gabe released his own pent-up load.

Gabe cleaned up, and rushed straight home to tell Alara what had happened. They were both equally as perplexed about what to do.

"Clearly the kid meant for you to get the DVD this time. You don't make a mistake like that twice," she said.

"I agree one hundred percent. But what do I do if he's sneaking me these videos and not showing his face?" Frustration showed through in Gabe's voice.

"Well, it's flattering that the kid wants you to see this stuff. Even if it is a little weird at the same time." Alara had a way of stating the obvious that helped to clarify situations. "I guess you just need to let him come to you when he's ready."

"Yeah, you're right. I mean, what else can I do?" Gabe sighed and his shoulders drooped.

That night in his apartment, Gabe watched the video again and jerked off one more time before going to bed. Sleep didn't come easily or peacefully. He tossed and turned and just kept thinking about this cute, adorable kid who was showing his adventurous side to Gabe. But, more than anything, Gabe realized he was jealous of this hung guy that Tommy had sucked off on camera.

The next few days were painful. Gabe kept hoping Tommy would come by the store and say something to him. At the same time, he was nervous too. What would he say if Tommy *did* approach him? Would Gabe admit to jacking off to the two videos? All he could do, like Alara said, was wait and see.

The days became weeks. Regular monitoring of the store's computer system showed that Tommy hadn't rented a movie, even on Gabe's days off. Gabe had managed to put Tommy out of his head for the most part. He even dug up the phone number of a guy he'd met months before named Alan, and arranged a date. Gabe figured the best way to forget about Tommy was to move on and see other guys, which sounded sort of funny when he thought about it. It was as if Gabe were trying to get over a break-up with a guy he barely knew anything about.

Well into the second month after seeing Tommy's second homemade DVD, Gabe began to stop worrying about it so much. He even stopped using the computer to watch for signs of activity on Tommy's account. He figured either Tommy was working hard at his new job or he felt embarrassed about being so brazen with his passive sharing of his sexual exhibitions. Whatever the case, Gabe was starting not to care.

Gabe had met Alan months before at a friend's house party, well before Tommy had come into the picture. They had exchanged numbers, but so far neither had called the other. When Alan answered the phone, he clearly hadn't expected it to be Gabe on the other end. Nonetheless, Alan seemed genuinely interested in meeting up for dinner. They planned for Alan to swing by the video store one night after Gabe had closed up. From there they would grab a late dinner and see where the night led them. Gabe was pretty sure that if he liked Alan, he'd flash him a few dimpled smirks and they'd end up back at Gabe's apartment for some horizontal fun.

That night, Gabe walked to the front door of the store and locked up. He grabbed the drop box of videos and headed back to the counter to enter them into the computer as returned. There weren't many movies in the box, which meant that Gabe might get finished early and have time to rush back into the staff bathroom and freshen up before Alan arrived.

As Gabe punched in the codes into the computer, it beeped and flashed the renter's account to signal it had recorded the return. Then Gabe grabbed the last one in the box and punched in the code. The computer beeped, and Tommy's account flashed on screen. Gabe froze.

"Fuck!"

What was he supposed to do now? This was the first time Tommy had rented a video in months, and Gabe had finally managed to stop thinking about Tommy. Gabe was afraid to open the case, but he had to. It was his job to make sure that the store's DVD was inside. He felt like he was moving in slow motion. He cracked open the case and closed his eyes. He lifted one eyelid and peeked, and there it was.

"Fuck fuck fuck!"

Another blank DVD was sitting on top of the store's movie. Gabe's head was spinning. What was he supposed to do? This could reignite all the craziness that had taken months to extinguish. Maybe he should just toss it in the trash and forget about it.

Just then, there was a soft knock on the front door. As crazy as it was, Gabe looked up half expecting to see Tommy standing there. Instead, Gabe saw Alan waving at him.

"Damn."

In the 90 seconds since seeing Tommy's account pop up on the screen, Gabe had completely forgotten about his date. He had to pull it together. He waved at Alan and signaled to him that he'd be two more minutes. Gabe went into the back room with Tommy's DVD in his hand. He dropped the DVD into his backpack and went to the sink. The cold water felt good as he splashed it on his face, and helped to snap him out of the sudden trance he'd fallen into.

Gabe reappeared a few minutes later, fresher and as

ready for his date as he could be. He opened the door, let himself out, and locked it again behind him.

"Hey Alan. Good to see you again."

"You too Gabe. Glad you called." They quickly gave each other a light hug. It was always good to establish a little bit of body contact early on in a date.

"So, where do you want to eat?" Alan asked.

"How about that new Thai place just up Castro? It's new and quiet, and I hear the food's great," Gabe suggested.

"Lead the way!"

They got a seat right away and chit-chatted while they waited for their meals. Over dinner they shared their stories about where they were from, where they worked, first boyfriends, etc. But Gabe was finding it hard to concentrate of anything Alan said. He felt as if he were on autopilot. All he could think about was the DVD in his bag.

"Gabe?"

"Huh, what?"

"I was waiting for you to respond to my question and you kind of just sat there staring blankly back at me. Are you okay?" Alan reached out and put his hand on Gabe's hand.

"Oh, yeah. Sorry about that. I had a crazy day at work. So, what was it that you asked again?" Gabe said with a sheepish grin. It still seemed that Alan was interested in him, so he didn't break out the dimples just yet.

They chatted some more and Gabe tried hard to concentrate. He didn't want to fuck up this date. At the same time, his mind kept drifting back to the images of Tommy waiting for him in his backpack. When the check came, Gabe paid and they left the restaurant. They wandered a few yards down from the restaurant and stopped on the sidewalk.

Gabe took a deep breath. "Alan, I had a great time, and you are super-cute. But I'm going to be honest; I had a tough day. I'd love to hang out some more. But I don't think I'd be much fun tonight," Gabe confessed.

"Okay. I appreciate you being honest. I was starting to wonder if you liked me, or if you were just going through the motions at dinner."

"No, I *do* like you. Who wouldn't like you? You're amazing. I hope we can we hang out again next week when I've had a chance to unwind. I promise I'm not trying to brush you off."

Alan blushed a little. "It's refreshing to have someone be honest like this. Give me a call next week and we'll get together again. Maybe on your day off?"

"Great!" smiled Gabe. And now was the time to deploy the big guns. "Can I offer you a kiss goodnight as a rain check?" Gabe's dimpled grin radiated across his face.

"I'd like that."

They kissed. It was a fantastic first date kiss. Just enough tongue to tempt and hint at things to come. About five seconds later, Gabe pulled back a little. Then reached in and gave Alan a peck on the lips and then the cheek.

"Thanks for understanding. I'm definitely looking forward to hanging out again when I'll be better company," Gabe said.

"Me too."

They said their goodbyes and Gabe turned to head home. He was so intent on getting home, he had to stop himself from running twice. He took the stairs to his third floor apartment two at a time. Once inside his apartment, he pulled out his laptop and the DVD, and popped it in. The movie came on the screen and showed about ten minutes of footage waited for him. Gabe hesitated with his hand over the play button. If he pressed play, he was reversing all the progress he'd made at forgetting about Tommy's crazy video sexcapades. But then again, who was he kidding? He'd already ended a date prematurely because of this DVD. He was still totally mesmerized by Tommy's allure.

"Fuck it," he said and pushed play.

Once again the screen immediately came alive with action. Tommy was lying facedown on a bed with his ass pushed up in the air. A random guy came into view and climbed onto the bed. Gabe peered closer to see if it was maybe the same guy from the previous video. Almost immediately Gabe knew it was not the same guy. This guy's dick was massive–bigger than the previous guy's member, and much larger than even Gabe's.

"Tell me what you want," Gabe heard the guy ask Tommy. Tommy mumbled something into the pillow.

"I can't hear you. I can't give you what you want if you don't tell me."

"I want you to fuck me," Tommy said, raising his head from the pillow. "Fuck me now. Please," he begged.

"That's all I needed to hear. Get ready, because here it comes."

With that, the top man inched closer to Tommy's upturned, muscled ass. The extra-hung top positioned his sheathed cock at the opening of Tommy's hole. As the top started to slide his cock in, Tommy pushed backward. The top grinned, and kept sliding forward. With half of his huge manhood buried in Tommy's ass, the top man stopped to let Tommy get used to his dick's girth and length. Tommy just wiggled and tried to push back further.

"Heh heh. Fuck kid; you really are a little slut. Well, let's see how much of my cock you can handle." With that, the top pushed forward, burying the full length of his thick dick up Tommy's butt in one quick stroke. Tommy lurched forward from the impact. His head came up and his back arched. Gabe thought he could hear Tommy mutter "Fuuuccck" through gritted teeth.

The top picked up speed, and was fucking Tommy deep. He pulled all the way out, and then slammed back in, balls deep. And to Gabe's surprise, Tommy was matching the top's speed and intensity. He'd rock forward on his knees and then slam his ass backwards as the top shoved his dick forward. This wasn't the innocent Tommy that Gabe had come to imagine in his head. It wasn't the Tommy who was too afraid to rent X-rated movies. This definitely wasn't the new kid who was impressed and intimidated by big city life. But then Gabe realized that that had all been in his own head; his own impressions that he'd projected onto Tommy.

"Spank me. Harder," Gabe suddenly heard Tommy demand. And then a loud clapping sound rang out as the top's big hand made contact with Tommy's ass.

"More! Don't stop. Please!" Tommy begged.

And the top seemed more than happy to oblige Tommy in his request. A few minutes later, Tommy's ass was bright red with handprints. Then the top stopped slapping Tommy's ass and grabbed onto each side of Tommy's hips with his hands. He started to pound deep and hard. The top started grunting and Tommy was gasping as he had the air knocked out of him with each powerful thrust.

Tommy pulled himself up somewhat more upright, back arched and supporting himself on one arm. With the other hand he reached down and started madly stroking his dick.

"Fuck me harder. Yeah. Yeah. I'm going to come," Tommy's voice went up a notch with each word.

And with a few final thrusts, the top fucked Tommy's load out of him. The first shot erupted out of Tommy's dick and shot past the bed's headboard, and onto the wall. The next several shots covered his pillows and sheets. Tommy collapsed forward, gasping for air, moaning and babbling incoherently. The top's dick was still buried deep in Tommy's hole. Slowly, he pulled back as if he might let the kid bask in his orgasmic stupor. But just as he reached near complete withdrawal, the top shoved his dick back in deep into Tommy's hole. Tommy didn't even seem to register the renewed invasion on his posterior.

The top fucked Tommy for a minute or so more,

before he pulled all the way out, ripped off the condom, and shot a sticky load all over Tommy's bright red ass. He rubbed his deflating cock up and down Tommy's ass crack, a few times, then spanked Tommy's ass hard one more time. The slap seemed to send a shock through Tommy's sensitive bottom, and he finally collapsed fully onto the bed.

"Kid, that was amazing. Not many guys can take a pounding like that from my cock. You call me again soon when you need more," the top said as he wiped his dick clean with the sheets and then walked out of the camera's view.

Gabe watched as Tommy's heaving, spent body lay there. Then Gabe took a deep breath of his own, guessing that he'd unknowingly been holding his breath during the last couple of minutes. The screen went blank and Gabe blinked a dozen or so times in a row. He started to come back to his own reality, realizing he was in his own room and sitting on his couch. He began to take note of his physical and mental state. His heart was racing and his breathing was quick and heavy. Then he also realized that his groin was warm and wet. He unzipped and stuck his hand down his pants. When he pulled it back out, it was covered in his own sticky jizz. Gabe had gotten off without touching himself while watching Tommy's ass get plowed.

"Fuckin' hell. What is this kid doing to me? This is so fucked up!" he said to himself and to no one at the same time.

"Hello?" Alara's voice sounded sleepy through the phone.

"Alara, hey it's me. I'm glad you're home. Did I wake you?" Gabe asked.

"I think I must've dozed off with a book in my hand and Trixie in my lap," she explained. "What's up sweetie? How was your date with Alan?"

"Um, yeah. The date. Well, that was okay. I sort of ended it early. Something else came up and was on my mind."

"Uh oh. Want to come down and tell me all about it?"

A few minutes later Gabe was sitting on Alara's couch. Trixie woke up long enough to wiggle over into Gabe's lap and fell promptly back to sleep. Gabe explained the details of the night.

"Well, sweet stuff. This sounds messed up. He shouldn't be messing with your head like this. At the same time, you should have just tossed that DVD straight into he trash. But that's beside the point now. You've seen it, and have to decide how you're going to respond."

"Well, there is one thing that I *could* do..." Gabe trailed off and pondered something privately.

"And what's that?"

"I could look up his phone number and address in the computer at work. Maybe I should call him or swing by his apartment and just confront him about all this craziness," Gabe said, laying out options he wasn't sure he was capable of following through with. "I could just see if he's okay, or I dunno. I have no idea what I'd say to him. This is just so fucking weird," he said, frustrated.

"Well, you do what you're comfortable with. But, don't forget to call Alan. Definitely *do not* ruin things with Alan because of this craziness that Tommy is putting you through."

"You're right. I know you're right." Gabe picked Trixie up from his lap and placed her next to him. Then he stood up from the couch and said, "Okay. I'll let you get back to bed. I'll keep you posted on what I end up doing."

They hugged and said their goodnights. Gabe climbed the stairs to back up to his apartment and went to bed upset and confused.

Gabe returned to his fanatical routine of checking the computer for activity on Tommy's account. Each night as he retrieved the drop box at closing time, he both hoped for and feared another DVD from Tommy. Night after night went by with no sign of Tommy. This time, though, Gabe couldn't put Tommy out of his head so easily. Finally, four nights after watching Tommy's most recent movie, Gabe looked up Tommy's info in the computer. He scribbled down the address and phone number onto a piece of scrap paper and tucked it into the front pouch of his backpack. At least he'd have the information in case he finally worked up the courage to confront Tommy.

Gabe called Alan and they set a date for Gabe's day off on Sunday. They met up outside of Gabe's apartment and decided to take a stroll through the Castro with no intention or destination. They chatted and Gabe was much more attentive to the conversation than he had been on their previous date. As they passed the gelato shop, they both decided that it was warm enough stop in and get a scoop.

As they walked, talked, and snacked on gelato, they decided it might be fun to head toward the park. Golden Gate Park was always fun to walk through on Sundays, because it was closed to car traffic. On their way up Haight Street toward the park, Gabe spotted someone vaguely familiar that was headed toward them. As the guy got closer, Gabe knew for sure it was Tommy. A chill of excitement and anxiety sent a shiver down his spine.

Tommy was now within twenty feet of Gabe and Alan. Alan seemed to be unfazed by Gabe's temporarily diverted attention, and continued telling the story of his travels through Europe after college. As Tommy passed by, Gabe noticed the dark circles under Tommy's eyes. Gabe smiled in Tommy's direction, changing his body language hoping that Tommy would give some sort of friendly acknowledgement. Instead, Tommy continued to stare vacantly ahead, and passed by without the slightest recognition of Gabe.

Gabe's shoulders fell, and his smile disappeared. He realized that Tommy was either fucking with him, or was seriously fucked up. Gabe walked a few more blocks with Alan, nodding and listening to Alan's story. From deep down, Gabe collected his wits, and scolded himself, "Don't fuck this up." By the time they reached the park, he had fully re-engaged with Alan. They walked the length of the park, talking, joking, laughing, and subtly making flirtatious body contact.

When they reached the ocean, they agreed to grab a cab back home. They'd had a fantastic day, and both agreed they should hang out again. Gabe was glad that Alan was content with taking things slow, and he was starting to like Alan, a lot. Gabe even thought it might be good for the development of their relationship to wait before having sex. Not that he'd ever tried that before to know for sure. But maybe now he was experiencing what it was like to have a grown-up relationship that started with platonic dates and that eventually led to an intensely intimate connection.

No matter how good things were with Alan, thoughts of Tommy still lingered in the back of Gabe's mind.

The relationship between Gabe and Alan grew steadily. After four dates and several weeks, they still hadn't slept together. The furthest they'd gotten was making out for a half-hour on Gabe's couch. That night Gabe could feel Alan's erection press against his own. Alan was the first to pull back from the kiss. He explained that despite how turned on he was, he still wanted to take things slowly. Gabe was incredibly intrigued by this, and admitted that he, too, was enjoying this new approach. Alan went home that night and Gabe fell asleep grinning about the fact that he was dating such an amazing guy.

A few days passed and on Saturday night, while Gabe was sitting bored at the store, his cell phone rang.

"Hello?"

"Hi hot stuff, it's Alan."

"Hey, what's up?"

"Well, I was wondering what you were doing tonight," prompted Alan. "I was thinking about it. And, you're so fucking great. I was hoping tonight we could take things to the next level, if you know what I mean..."

Gabe's cock sprang to attention. "Hell yes! I mean, er... Yeah, that sounds great."

"Glad you're as excited as I am. I'll swing by the store when you close and then we can head back to your place." Gabe liked that Alan was so direct and didn't beat around the bush.

"Cool, looking forward to it!" Gabe hung up the phone. Because the store was empty, he did a little happy dance behind the counter. The rest of the day he couldn't stop thinking about Alan, and how amazing it was going to be to connect with him on a physical level that night.

The day dragged on predictably, and Gabe rushed through his closing chores. He considered leaving the drop box movies for the morning shift. He wanted to be ready when Alan arrived. But, he was so filled with energy that he decided he would zip through them. He checked in 20 movies and had only a few more to go when Tommy's account flashed on the screen.

"God damn you. Fuck you, Tommy," Gabe yelled at the computer screen, which was the closest thing Gabe had to an interaction with Tommy.

Gabe angrily opened the jewel case. Sure enough, there was another blank DVD inside. Gabe couldn't figure out how Tommy managed to pick the absolute worst nights to deliver these videos.

Gabe grabbed the DVD from the jewel case and stared at it. Something was different. Not with the blank DVD–that still looked exactly like they always did. No, something was different inside of him. He realized that he *didn't care* about the DVD this time. Something had changed in the way he thought about Tommy. Maybe it was Tommy's complete lack of acknowledgement on the street that day. Maybe it was being in such a great relationship with Alan. Or maybe it was the promise of long-anticipated sex with Alan that night. Whatever it was, Gabe was indifferent about the DVD he held in his hand. And, he was just about to toss it in the wastebasket when he heard the door open.

"You ready?" It was Alan. Gabe realized that in his excitement he must've forgotten to lock the door.

"Oh hey, you startled me a little. I guess I forgot to lock up earlier. Must be all the anticipation..." Gabe said.

"What's that in your hand?" asked Alan innocently.

"Oh this? Nothing. Somebody must've left it in the DVD case by accident." Gabe moved toward the wastebasket.

"Wait, you're going to throw it away? Aren't you going to keep it in case someone wants it back? What if it's a video of somebody's kid's first steps?" Alan was such sweetheart and Gabe didn't want to try to explain what it was that he had in his hand.

"You're right. I'll just stash it in back while I grab my stuff. Be right out, and then we can head back to my place."

"That's what I was hoping you'd say," said Alan with a big smile on his face.

Back at Gabe's apartment, the two men couldn't keep themselves off of each other. They rubbed and kissed and caressed. Gabe enjoyed the playful game they started where they each got to pick the next item of clothing they stripped off the other. With not much clothing left, Gabe and Alan were rock hard and rubbing their erect members against each other through light cotton boxers.

Their passion marched steadily forward, until they were naked in Gabe's bed, bodies pressed firmly together as they kissed. Gabe could feel Alan's body heat transfer to his own skin. Alan loved the way Gabe's dick pulsed against his stomach when they kissed. Gabe reached for the nightstand and pulled out a condom and some lube.

"I hope there's enough in there for you and me both," Alan said with a smirk.

"Um, well, I uh...I don't usually bottom," Gabe said, not wanting to kill the mood.

Alan laughed. "Yeah, well, neither do I. But I figure if I'm going to take that big thing up my butt, you should return the favor."

"Let's just see what happens." Gabe hadn't bottomed in years, and hoped he might be able to distract Alan with Gabe's own special topping moves.

The sex was intense and Gabe had never felt more intimately connected to another human being. Alan anticipated Gabe's every move, meeting his thrusts, twisting and switching positions at the slightest indication from Gabe. It was intense and mind blowing and passionate. Gabe wanted to be buried deep in Alan's ass for the rest of his life. Unfortunately, the pleasure was just too great, and Gabe unloaded into the condom deep inside Alan's ass. As if on cue, Alan's own dick erupted simultaneously.

The two men lay there on the bed, cuddling and staring at the ceiling. They nuzzled each other and occasionally gave each other a loving peck on the forehead or cheek. Their breathing and heart rates eventually returned to normal, and Gabe pulled Alan closer into his embrace. Gabe gently ran his hands over Alan's lightly hairy chest and down his impressively rippled abs. Moving even further south, Gabe felt Alan's cock fully recovered and engorged.

"My turn?" Alan asked and then kissed Gabe hard on the mouth. Eyes closed, their tongues danced together in unison. Alan felt something brush against his arm. He opened his eyes and saw that Gabe was holding a condom out for Alan.

Their lips parted and Gabe said, "Just go easy on me, okay?"

Alan simply smiled as he took the condom and positioned himself over Gabe.

***

Neither Alan nor Gabe had to work the next morning, so they slept in late. When Gabe groggily opened his eyes, Alan was still spooning him from behind. Gabe was sore from bottoming the night before. Twice. He also felt content and fulfilled, lying there in the arms of someone who was so fantastic. He wanted to lie there in Alan's arms all day. And, as he realized it was Sunday and he didn't have to work, he probably could stay right there if he really wanted too.

Eventually Alan woke up and they took turns getting each other off with blowjobs. In the shower, the kissed and playfully grabbed at each other's asses and dicks. After brunch, Alan finally kissed Gabe goodbye and went back to his own place to take care of some chores with a promise to meet back up in a day or two.

All week Gabe felt like he was walking on rainbows. The sun seemed brighter, the air smelled sweeter, birds were chirping love songs; love was literally in the air. Gabe and Alan made love twice more that week and they seemed to be falling into a serious relationship. The best part for Gabe was that they enjoyed each other's company out of the bedroom as much as they enjoyed taking turns fucking each other between the sheets.

On Sunday, a full week later, Gabe was home doing chores and laundry. Alan was going to come over that night to watch *Pirates of the Caribbean* at Gabe's house. It had just come out on DVD and both Alan and Gabe thought Orlando Bloom was dreamy. Gabe's backpack sat on his couch, and he grabbed it to move it aside so that he could straighten up. As he shifted the backpack, the unzipped pouch spilled out his laptop and a few other things.

Gabe started to pick up the various items and froze. He was holding Tommy's most recent DVD. It had been over a week since he'd stuffed the DVD into his backpack. And, because he'd been in such a daze of relationship bliss, he'd forgotten all about it.

"Oh man..." Gabe sighed. "What the hell am I

supposed to do with this?"

Gabe picked up the phone and called Alara. He explained the situation and she was knocking on his door a few minutes later. Gabe opened the door and Alara walked in, followed by the clickity-clack of Trixie's prancing toenails.

"So, should I watch it?" Gabe asked. "Or should I just dump it in the trash?"

"That's a tough one. Even I'm a little curious to see what he sent you this time," Alara said as she sat on the couch. Trixie jumped up in her lap.

"Would you watch it with me?" Gabe asked. "If you watch it with me, you can always just tell me to stop watching if it gets out of hand."

"All right, I'm not sure that's any better, but I'm too curious to say no."

Gabe popped the DVD into his laptop and hovered his hand over the play button. "Here we go," he said and pressed play.

Both Alara and Gabe were immediately stunned by what they saw. Tommy was facedown on a bed, arms bound behind him with ass up in the air. He was blindfolded and his ass was already bright red from being spanked.

Alara brought her hand to her mouth. "Gabe, this is different than the other ones, right?"

"Yeah, this is definitely different."

They continued to watch as a naked guy with a mask got on the bed and spanked Tommy's ass hard. The resounding smack and the sight of Tommy's shuddering body made both Alara and Gabe flinch. They watched as the top shoved his uncovered dick into Tommy's ass and fucked him brutally. On screen, Gabe could barely detect a reaction from Tommy. After a few minutes the top pulled out and shot a load all over Tommy's ass and back. He rubbed his come all over Tommy's ass cheeks and started spanking them again. Tommy shivered each time a hand made contact with his sensitive butt.

"You're a dirty little slut. And you know what dirty

little sluts need?" The top growled at Tommy. "They need to be cleaned up."

The top then took hold of his now-soft cock and began pissing all over Tommy's back and ass. After he'd emptied his bladder, the top pulled at the knot on Tommy's arm restraints and Tommy's arms fell to his sides. The top got off the bed and exited the room. Tommy just laid there shaking. After a minute, he pulled himself up and removed the blindfold. Gabe hardly recognized the thin boy walking toward the camera. His eyes were hollow, as if they'd lost their connection to his soul. Tears were streaming silently down from Tommy's eyes. As he reached for the camera to turn it off, he closed his eyes and gritted his teeth. Then the camera screen went black.

"Gabe, you have to call him. He needs help." Alara had fear in her voice.

"Fuck, I know. I'm one step ahead of you." Gabe was already reaching for his backpack where he remembered stashing Tommy's phone number. He retrieved the scrap of paper and dialed. It rang five times before going to voicemail. The voice on the outgoing greeting was the Tommy that Gabe remembered meeting many months ago.

"Hi, this is Tommy. I'm probably working or off exploring this great city. Leave me a message and I promise, I'll get back to you as soon as I can. Thanks for calling!"

Gabe waited for the beep. "Tommy, this is Gabe. I need to talk to you. Please call me. Or stop by the store." He left his phone number and hung up.

"Alara, will you go over to his house with me?" Gabe was staring at the piece of paper that also had Tommy's address on it. "We have to see if he's all right."

"Of course. Let me put some shoes on. I'll meet you in the lobby in ten minutes."

They walked the few blocks to Tommy's apartment building and rang the buzzer for his apartment. There was no answer. They rang it again and again. Just as they were about to ring it a fourth time, one of Tommy's fellow apartment building tenants exited the main lobby door. Alara grabbed the door and they both let themselves inside. They walked up to the fourth floor and found Tommy's apartment number. They knocked and waited. There was no response. They knocked some more and tried the doorknob. It was locked.

A neighbor's door opened and a woman in her fifties emerged. She saw Gabe and Alara standing in front of Tommy's door and nodded in their direction.

"He's not home. Cute kid. I used to see him every morning on his way to work. Haven't seen him since mid-last week though. Figured he must've gone out of town or something," she explained. "Are you his friends?"

"Yeah, we thought he'd be home. We're concerned about him. It's probably nothing, but if you see him, could you call me?" Gabe scribbled his name and number on some paper he pulled from his backpack and handed it to the woman.

"I certainly will. I hope nothing's wrong."

"Me too," said Gabe, a slight trace of worry in his voice.

Gabe and Alara left the apartment building and went back home. Gabe parted ways with Alara on her floor and promised to tell her if he heard anything. He tried calling Tommy a dozen more times that day, and stopped back by his apartment twice more. Every day over the following week, Gabe stopped by Tommy's apartment on the way to and from work and tried the buzzer with no luck.

Then on Friday, as Gabe stopped at Tommy's place on his way to work, he noticed a moving truck in front of Tommy's apartment building. Gabe approached one of the movers and asked what apartment they were moving. Not seeing any reason to hold back details, the mover indicated the apartment number. It was Tommy's.

Gabe let himself in through the propped open lobby door and went upstairs to Tommy's floor. He peeked inside and noticed that the small apartment was empty. The moving company manager was standing there checking off things on a clipboard.

"Excuse me. Um, do you know where this stuff is going?" Gabe asked, trying to not sound too nosy.

The manager seemed equally candid as his employee downstairs, "Don't know much about it. We got a request from someone in Cleveland to move the entire contents of this apartment. We're supposed to box everything up and ship it back to Cleveland." The manager mentioned two names that Gabe assumed were Tommy's parents.

"All right, thanks for your help," Gabe said as he nodded and left the room.

He had more details but no more answers. Gabe was still unsettled about Tommy vanishing from the city, especially not after the content of the last video Tommy had made. Gabe went to work and tried to figure out how to find out if Tommy was okay. He hoped that Tommy had finally just had too much and moved back to live with his parents. Maybe he'd left the city to ground himself and get his head back on straight.

Saturday night Alan stopped by the store and picked Gabe up for a dinner date. They went back to Gabe's place, had sex, and fell asleep holding each other. When Gabe woke up, he slowly extracted himself from Alan's embrace without waking his new lover. Gabe put on pair of shorts, a t-shirt, and some sneakers and went downstairs to buy a Sunday paper. By the time he got back upstairs, Alan was up, and cooking them breakfast.

"Nice moves getting out of bed without waking me." Alan winked at Gabe.

"Thanks, it's one of my many talents." Gabe leaned in and kissed Alan.

"Mmmm. I know. Many, many talents," Alan said

breaking off from the kiss and grabbing Gabe's cute ass.

Gabe sat down at the kitchen table and opened the newspaper. He flipped through various sections, reading out loud interesting tidbits to Alan.

"Breakfast's almost ready, so put that away," Alan instructed.

Gabe thumbed through the last section of the paper. He was mostly skimming through just to feel like he'd gotten his money's worth. He turned the last page to the obituaries. He let out a little cry of shock as his stomach sank. Tears filled his eyes. There on the page was Tommy's name.

Gabe read Tommy's obituary. A body had been found floating in the bay. It was suspected that Tommy had jumped from the Golden Gate Bridge in the middle of the night a week earlier. His body had been discovered in the morning by Coast Guard patrols a week prior. No next of kin were listed, and no suicide note had been discovered. And that was it.

Alan came over to stand behind Gabe, sensing that something was wrong. He put his hand on Gabe's shoulder. Just then, Gabe turned in his seat; his body went limp, and he collapsed onto the floor. Alan caught him in his arms and sat down on the floor with Gabe, holding him and rocking with him. Gabe sobbed uncontrollably.

"Gabe, what's wrong. What happened?" Alan was at a loss. He had no idea what could have upset Gabe this much.

They sat like this for twenty minutes before Gabe's sobs finally subsided enough for him to start verbalizing his grief. He told Alan everything, falteringly, as he sobbed through the tale.

"They said...they didn't find a suicide note," Gabe said through choked tears.

"Okay. I guess that is somewhat unusual," Alan said, not knowing exactly what to say.

"I think...it was...I think the last DVD was his suicide note." Gabe collapsed into Alan's arms, a complete mess of emotions and guilt.

Gabe's eyes were shut tightly as he cried into Alan's chest. He couldn't get the vision of the cute, adorable, innocent Tommy out of his head. The Tommy that walked into the store that day that was so flustered and excited by the city. Gabe kept crying and thinking to himself, "If only I'd watched it a week ago. If only I'd reached out sooner..."

The End

Extraordinary

Emily-Jean MacKenzie

Ryan remembered his first sexual experience with a man as though it were yesterday. It was clichéd as hell, taking place in the bathroom of a gay club with Diana Ross as the soundtrack. He was twenty years old. He didn't even get the name of the guy he was with, but he was significantly older. They'd ground together on the dance floor, sharing open-mouthed kisses and not-so-covert gropes before dragging one another off to the relative privacy of a restroom stall.

He sucked the guy's cock a little, and the guy sucked his, before Ryan watched him lean over against the wall, offering himself. Ryan didn't refuse. A little lube, a condom and Ryan didn't feel like such a virgin anymore. He'd fucked girls before, of course, but that had never seemed to count in his mind. It was just too ordinary.

It didn't last long, but it blew Ryan's mind, and from that moment on, he knew there was no turning back.

His first sexual experience with Elliott was barely worth mentioning in comparison. They'd shared a very grown-up dinner in a very grown-up restaurant before Elliott had invited Ryan back to his very grown-up apartment. It was spotless, all of his furniture matched, and his CDs were alphabetized. Ryan kind of wanted to run away. He didn't though. He stayed and he had a glass of wine and he fucked Elliott on his orthopedic mattress. The sex was nice, but it wasn't extraordinary. Ryan can't quite remember to this day why he bothered with a second date.

They fell in love somewhere in the next few months. It wasn't what Ryan intended. He thought he had a few more years of hot fucks and crazy nights before he settled down with someone and gave all of that up. He felt kind of like he'd been cut off in his prime. But he had no intention of leaving Elliott, so he resigned himself to the fact that there would be a lot more nights spent at home in his future.

Over the next few years, Elliott learned to loosen up a little, and Ryan learned to calm down. They met somewhere in the middle, and Ryan never felt as though he'd compromised anything to get there. That was when he realized that he was probably a grown-up too.

Their sex lives improved as Ryan showed the sheltered Elliott how to ride his dick, or how to have sex in locations other than the bed, or exactly what it felt like to have someone's tongue up his ass. Elliott seemed to enjoy the education. They would never have the kind of dirty fucks that Ryan had enjoyed during his early twenties, but he was 35 now, so he should probably be over that anyway. Life moved on. You had to keep moving with it.

Then, one Friday evening, Ryan's world was turned on its head.

They were still sticky and slightly breathless, the sheets only partially covering their bodies, as they lay bunched up together in the middle of the bed. Ryan's skin tingled in a strange way as he tried to comprehend what Elliott was telling him.

"You're serious?" he asked eventually, his voice coming out far more incredulous than he intended.

"I know this guy at work," Elliott said, his voice quiet and almost shy. "I think he'd be willing."

Ryan sat up, dislodging Elliott slightly. Elliott looked up at him, his eyebrows knitted in concern. Ryan just stared at him.

"You're serious?"

"You don't want to do it," Elliott said. There was

no question there, just resignation. "That's fine. Just say you don't want to do it. It was only a suggestion. A thought I had."

"A thought you had?" Ryan repeated. "You're Elliott. You don't have thoughts like that."

Elliott sighed. His mouth turned slightly downwards. "Forget I said anything." He shifted away from Ryan, just a little, but enough to get his point across.

"I'm sorry," Ryan offered. "I just...You're *Elliott*," he said again helplessly.

Elliott rolled his eyes.

"Oh, come on, you think it's kinky to do it on the floor," Ryan said.

"I think it's disgusting," Elliott said. "Do you know how much dirt there is stored up in a carpet?"

Ryan chose to ignore that last remark for the purposes of getting this conversation over with somewhere in the near future. "I'm just surprised," he said. "You gotta admit, this kinda came outta nowhere, El."

"I've always liked the thought of it," Elliott said with something like a shrug. "Two guys at once. Three of us together. It's hot."

"Damn fucking right it is," Ryan agreed, moving closer to him again. Elliott didn't try to move away.

"And I hardly thought I was going to shock you. You've done stuff like this before."

"Are you sure?" Ryan asked. "Because you can't take it back once you've done it."

"I'm a grown up, Ryan," Elliott stated, his tone of voice back on secure footing with that comment.

"Well, I'm game," Ryan told him, pressing his body against Elliott's and kissing him on the back of the neck.

Elliott made all of the arrangements. Ryan wanted to ask how that worked, how you approached your colleague and enquired whether they'd like to have a threeway with you and your boyfriend. He bet that

Elliott stammered over every word, unable to make eye contact. He kind of loved that image.

Luke came around one Saturday night. Ryan vaguely recognized him from the company picnic, and similar boring social events at Elliott's office, but he didn't think he'd ever spoken to him before. He was glad about that. There was nothing worse than trying to fuck someone you knew in passing. You always knew just enough about each other to make it horribly awkward.

He was pretty tall, tanned, his hair sun-kissed like he'd just been on vacation somewhere tropical. It was a contrast to both him and Elliott with their dark hair and bodies that barely saw the sun in their city apartment. Luke's skin, by comparison, looked warm to the touch. Ryan wondered what he looked like naked.

"Do you want a drink?" Elliott offered. "I could open a bottle of wine."

"How about some whiskey?" Ryan suggested. "Higher alcohol content in less time."

Elliott gave him a look like he was being uncivilized. Ryan was tempted to roll his eyes.

"Whiskey sounds good," Luke said.

Elliott nodded. He seemed a little thrown. "Yeah, okay," he said. "I'll be right back." He headed out to the kitchen. Ryan turned to look at Luke.

"Hey, listen, about tonight," he began. Luke turned to face him, mild concern written over his features. "I mean, nothing's out of bounds, and I'm totally into everything, but I thought it might be cool if we focused on Elliott tonight. He's never done anything like this before. It's kind of a little fantasy he's been harboring since he was twelve or something, so..."

Luke nodded, smiling slightly. "Got it."

Ryan looked away, his eyes flicking around the room before he focused on Luke again. "Seriously though, I am into pretty much anything. And I wanna have a little fun too."

Luke gave Ryan a look that went straight to his

cock. Elliott returned with the drinks.

"Okay, whiskey," he said, trying to sound sure of himself, but failing miserably. He handed the drinks out and then hesitated for a moment about where to sit, his eyes flicking between Ryan and Luke. He sat next to Ryan.

There was an awkward silence then, and the whole thing seemed horribly contrived. Ryan had done this before, but not in such an organized or grown-up manner. This is what life with Elliott did to him.

Elliott and Luke sipped their drinks politely. Ryan downed his and thought about nights when he'd picked up two guys at once from some shitty club and gone home with them in a haze of lust and alcohol and greed, everyone wanting everything now. He could see already that this experience was going to be worlds away from that.

He placed his empty glass down on the table and then leaned into Elliott, holding the side of his face and pulling him in for a kiss. It was slow, but it wasn't chaste. He pushed his tongue past Elliott's lips, tasting that clean, fresh taste that was Elliott. It kind of summed him up. Elliott responded in kind, tilting his head and kissing Ryan deeper, letting their tongues slide over one another. It made Ryan warmer all over.

As he pulled back, he looked into Elliott's eyes, rubbing a thumb over his cheek gently, before his gaze fell down to parted lips that were so inviting. Lips that you couldn't help but think about pushing your tongue past. Ryan brushed his mouth against Elliott's once more, and then he turned his attention to Luke.

Luke's eyes were dark. As Ryan stood up and walked towards him, they got darker still. Ryan could practically feel the sexual tension pressing down against his skin. It was beautiful. It was a bubble that they'd created between the three of them.

He let himself fall heavily to Luke's side and resisted the urge to look at Elliott before he joined his lips with Luke's. This kiss went slower, two unfamiliar styles trying to find common ground. It had been a long time since Ryan had kissed anyone new and he was surprised by how utterly alien it felt to have lips against his own that weren't Elliott's. He didn't think about these things anymore.

Luke tasted much stronger than Elliott ever did, but Ryan couldn't quite put his finger on what it was. Something almost woody. And he kissed more aggressively, if only a little. Elliott had a tendency to be gentle, even when he was being unashamedly passionate. He was always delicate and exploring, never rushed. Luke opened his mouth a fraction too wide as his tongue played against Ryan's, making it hard for Ryan to feel as though he were truly connecting. Even so, he could tell right away that Luke wasn't a bad kisser. Just different. He pulled back, looking him briefly up and down and wondering what else he did differently.

When he turned back to Elliott, it was with slight apprehension. He wasn't entirely sure how Elliott was going to take the reality of his boyfriend making out with someone else. These things often seemed a lot more attractive in theory.

Meeting Elliott's eyes, he could see that he was wrong. There was a certain uneasiness there, some nerves and too many sensible thoughts, but he was turned on. He was in. Ryan smiled at him and Elliott smiled back.

"C'mere," Ryan told him, nodding his head towards the space at the other side of Luke.

Elliott held his gaze as he walked across the room.

As their lips met, it seemed to take a while for Elliott to be willing to open his mouth to Luke, keeping his lips pressed together as he moved them against Luke's in an approximation of a kiss. Ryan smiled. It was quite endearing. When Elliott finally allowed Luke admittance, he did that same tilt of the head that he always did with Ryan. He let Luke lead. He seemed unsure where to put his hands. As the two of them pulled apart, Elliott's eyes instantly found Ryan's, seeking reassurance. Ryan gave it effortlessly with a smile and a smoldering look.

"Well, that's the introductions out of the way," Ryan said. "How about we take this to the bedroom, boys?"

The sheets on the bed had just been changed and they smelled of laundry detergent and high thread counts. Ryan took Elliott's hand and pulled him down onto the bed with him so that the pair were lying side by side. He looked to Luke, pointing out the empty spot beside Elliott and waiting for him to lie down with them. As the three of them were finally settled on the bed, still fully clothed, Ryan couldn't help but think that this was taking far too long. He was at a slight loss how to get things started. When he'd done these things in the past, he didn't make it to the bed with anyone until the desperation had already peaked. They were all a little too far away from that point right now.

In an attempt to rectify the situation, Ryan reached down, cupping Elliott through the soft fabric of his pants. He squeezed the outline of his dick, curling his fingers around it as Elliott made a small noise of appreciation in his throat. Ryan rubbed his hand back and forth, starting to feel Elliott harden under his touch as he caught Luke's eye. They stared at each other, dark eyes and anticipation, before Ryan reached out, directing Luke's hand to be in place of his own.

Elliott groaned, and Ryan wondered if Luke was doing something different than what he was doing. Something better. It was a strange feeling. He'd never tried anything like this with someone he'd cared about before. In truth, he'd never felt about anyone the way he felt about Elliott, so he'd never had the chance.

It was an experience though, and Ryan had never shied away from experiences, so he embraced what was happening and he let himself get turned on by the sight of his boyfriend and a man who was practically a complete stranger. It wasn't difficult. Elliott's mouth was open, his breath uneven, his cheeks flushed, and it pushed more than a few of Ryan's buttons, even if he wasn't the one in the driver's seat right now.

Ryan leaned down and captured Elliott's parted lips, pushing his tongue inside and running it slowly over Elliott's own. This time, Ryan knew that the moan was for him. He could feel Elliott's body swelling slightly upwards towards Luke's hand as he allowed Ryan to kiss him deeply, his hands clinging to Ryan, one fisted in his shirt and the other hooked securely around his neck.

The momentum seemed to change slightly as Ryan was aware of Luke leaning down too, his mouth against Elliott's neck. Elliott made a noise that sounded almost confused, and Ryan was tempted to feel sorry for him. Elliott was the kind of guy who couldn't watch porn and make out at the same time because he felt like there was too much going on. Ryan could only imagine how he was handling this. But that was the point. Elliott had asked. Elliott wanted to find out. Ryan was going to make sure that he did.

He felt Elliott relaxing into it more, his mouth opening wider to Ryan, his tongue actively seeking Ryan's out where he'd previously simply let himself be kissed. His hand slackened off on Ryan's shirt and then it disappeared completely, clearly holding onto Luke in some way instead. He was welcoming them both. He was finding his feet and taking what he wanted. Ryan kind of loved him for that.

Their bodies moved closer together until Ryan felt as though he could feel Luke touching him through Elliott. He pressed himself up against Elliott's side, pushing his hard-on against Elliott's thigh through layers of denim and cotton. He felt warm all over in the best possible way. It wasn't the kind of heat that you got through horniness and frustration and need. It was the kind of heat that steadily grew within, building into something more wonderful than that sense of urgency that had been so familiar to Ryan in the past. It was the kind of heat he'd only ever gotten with Elliott.

He left Elliott's mouth with a final lick and pulled back, looking down at him. Elliott looked back, his eyes full of so much want that it made Ryan want to dive right back in again. Instead, he watched Luke for a moment, the way that his mouth played over Elliott's neck, the way that he licked and sucked and nipped at the flesh. It was incredibly hot. So was that misty look in Elliott's eyes.

Elliott had dressed to impress tonight, wearing an expensive, button down shirt and a pair of black slacks. He did look good. He looked delicious, the subtle hint of aftershave finishing off the ensemble. But it was far too formal for the occasion really, and Ryan cursed the tiny buttons as he started to undo them. Elliott was the kind of person who cared about appearances, how things looked from the outside. He wasn't vain, like Ryan knew that he had a tendency to be. He was just overly concerned with first impressions. One of his many preoccupations in life that stopped him ever truly letting go.

As more and more of Elliott's flesh was revealed, Luke's mouth moved lower, following Ryan's hands. Elliott arched his back up towards that mouth, silently asking for more. Some tiny voice in Ryan's head told him that he should be jealous, but he wasn't. Not quite. He knew that he could do to Elliott exactly what Luke was doing and more. He never got to see what that looked like though. He never got to see Elliott slide down further into his own lust until he was overtaken with it. Ryan was always too busy sliding with him. Right now, he could see what a wonderful opportunity he had in front of him.

"Do you want to suck his cock?" Ryan asked. Luke lifted his head to look at him. Elliott looked up too. "It's a really nice cock."

There was silence. Not really silence. There was heavy breathing and pounding hearts.

"Yeah, reckon I would," Luke finally said.

Elliott made a small noise that seemed entirely involuntary. Ryan smiled at Luke and then worked Elliott's pants open for him. He yanked them down his legs as Luke moved towards Elliott's dick that jutted out from his body, eager and ready. Ryan sat by Elliott's side and watched. Luke lowered his mouth around Elliott's cock.

There was a kind of electricity in the room that Ryan felt like an intrinsic part of, even if in reality he was only an observer. But Elliott made him feel like so much more than that as he reached out clumsily and looked into his eyes while he moaned at the feel of what Luke was doing to him. Ryan held onto his hand and then his gaze fell downwards, watching Luke's red lips move up and down Elliott's cock. It made Ryan's own dick throb.

Elliott's body seemed to pulse, as though controlled by some outside force. His hips rode up towards Luke's mouth, and Ryan was amazed by how fluid it looked. He didn't seem to be putting any effort in. His body was liquid, on ocean surging upwards and falling back down towards the seabed, the tide smoothly pulling in everything around it.

Ryan reached down, touching the side of Luke's face, feeling his slightly hollowed cheek under his fingertips. Luke's eyes raised up to him, pupils blown wide, his head still bobbing up and down on Elliott's dick. His skin felt hot. They simply looked at each other for a few loaded moments, sharing the secrets of Elliott's body, before Ryan's fingers curled into a grip and he pulled Luke's lips away from Elliott, their mouths colliding with one another over Elliott's body.

Slipping his tongue into Luke's mouth now, Ryan noted that he tasted different. He tasted of Elliott. It was peculiar, tasting Elliott's unique flavors second hand from someone else. It was also incredibly erotic. Something so familiar and so sordid all at once.

They kissed and they touched and they finally undressed one another, Elliott lying between and below them. Luke's body was hard and tight and it was obvious that he worked out, like Elliott did. Ryan had never been in a gym in his life, and he didn't think that his physique had particularly suffered for it. Elliott had tried to drag him along on more than a couple of occasions, but Ryan always had something better to do. He couldn't think of anything more tedious and exhausting than pumping iron or running on the spot or pretending to row a boat. That didn't mean he couldn't appreciate the results in other people, though. As he ran his hands over Luke's abs, he swayed heavily towards him, undeniably turned on by the firmness and the warmth.

By the time they were all naked, Ryan could tell that the atmosphere was exactly where it needed to be. It was still different to all of the times that Ryan had done similar things, nowhere near as spontaneous or desperate or casual, but it was clear that the formalities were out of the way. Now they were just three guys, three grown-ups, and the careful etiquette of earlier was forgotten in favor of finding satisfaction, for themselves and for each other.

Ryan dropped down onto the bed beside Elliott, capturing his mouth and kissing him deeply. Their tongues tangled and their hands grabbed, pulling one another irresistibly closer as their naked bodies pressed together through a sheen of sweat. Ryan rubbed against him, building a friction that they easily lost themselves to, moans and groans captured between them. It was what Ryan had always termed intimate and private between he and Elliott, something special and just for them, and yet the knowledge that Luke's eyes were bearing witness to this act made Ryan even hotter. He didn't try to make sense of that.

They rolled, Elliott on top of Ryan, and Ryan held him there. It was hard to breathe with Elliott's tongue in his mouth and his weight pressed firmly down against his chest. He didn't stop though, didn't let up. If anything, he forced them closer, tighter, deeper. It made the headrush worthwhile. It made Ryan's dick harder. He took it all in for as long as he could stand and then he ripped his mouth away and gasped for air. Focusing on Elliott's eyes seemed to take longer than he intended.

"Hands and knees."

He meant to sound commanding and in control and sure of himself, but he realized as he ran his hands absently over Elliott's body that he was none of those things. He'd long since past that point.

"Wha'?" Elliott slurred. Elliott wasn't the kind of man who slurred, and so Ryan took comfort in the fact that Elliott was clearly as far gone as him.

"Want you on your hands and knees," Ryan tried again. "Over me."

Elliott's eyes flitted around slightly with uncertainty. "Why?"

Ryan made sure that Elliott was looking right at him as he said the next words. "Because I want to watch you get fucked."

Elliott whimpered. Ryan brushed their lips together and then turned to Luke who was laid by his side. He tilted his head over, Luke bridging the gap and joining their mouths. The kiss was almost like the breathless one he shared with Elliott, and yet, at the same time, it was a world away. Ryan loved that duality. He loved that the same act could mean two completely different things. Neither was really any better than the other in the moment. The contrast merely heightened everything.

"Condoms and lube are on the side," he said against Luke's lips as they pulled apart. His voice was dark with want and desire. He even turned himself on a little with it.

Luke moved, and then Elliott moved too, hoisting himself unsteadily onto all fours over Ryan's body. He swayed slightly as Luke knelt behind him, flipping open the lube. Ryan had never felt so detached from that sound before. Elliott looked down at him, brown eyes

wide and slightly moist, so clearly overwhelmed by
what was happening. It was beautiful and it made Ryan
feel a little bit overwhelmed too.

As Luke's fingers slid inside him, Elliott kept his
gaze focused firmly on Ryan's, sharing it with him. He
gave a stifled moan, his hands gripping the sheets at
either side of Ryan's body, and Ryan found himself
wishing that those fingers were digging into his flesh
instead of the expensive linen.

But this is what he wanted. To be an observer. To
be objective. He'd never seen Elliott get fucked before,
never knew what it looked like. He'd fucked Elliott of
course, but that was different. In those moments, he
was usually too busy feeling Elliott's insides around his
cock to really see him. Watching was new. It had never
occurred to him before, but from the second he saw
Elliott react to Luke's touch, the plan had formed so
firmly in his mind. He needed this. He needed to watch
Elliott come undone in a way that he never could when
he was losing it with him.

Elliott's eyelids became heavy, his gaze unseeing,
but still on Ryan. He was panting, his fair cheeks
dappled with pink, his arms shaking just the tiniest bit.
Ryan couldn't see what Luke was doing from where he
lay, not with any great accuracy, but he could see the
sensations as they ran through Elliott's body, and that
was what he really cared about. He could guess at
everything else.

As Luke finally pushed his cock into Elliott's body,
Elliott shuddered from head to toe, scarcely keeping
hold of himself. His eyes closed fully and his hips tilted
upwards in an undeniably inviting gesture. Luke curled
his fingers around those hips, holding him tight as he
leant over him and got himself into a better position,
inadvertently giving Ryan a wonderful view.

He could see them both, see the contrast, Elliott's
pale, flushed skin against Luke's gentle tan, Elliott's
dark hair against Luke's pale, messed-up strands. He
could see the similarities too, see how they both took

care of themselves, how they both enjoyed control, and how they were both so clearly losing it right now. It excited Ryan. It made him want to touch himself, made him want to touch them. He didn't do either though, not yet. Instead, he stayed still and watched as their bodies found an irresistible rhythm of push and pull that Ryan found almost hypnotizing.

The room was filled with sex that was so much more tangible than the simple act. There was the sound of it, the grunts and groans from Elliott and Luke. And then there was the smell, heady and manly and strong. It was only a matter of time before Ryan found himself giving in to the touch too, reaching out and stroking the side of Elliott's face. Elliott jumped slightly, his eyes opening and drawing Ryan in. Ryan let his hand run down over the heated flesh, feeling Elliott's chest and abdomen, before his fingers finally found his swollen cock, closing around it and giving a squeeze. He felt it jump in his hand as Elliott's body tensed, and he thought he was going to come right there.

The rhythm of their hips was steady, but slightly rushed. Ryan found it easily enough, matching it with his hand as it slid on pearly pre-come, making everything so wonderfully fluid. Elliott's eyes shut again, screwing tightly closed, and his body buffeted from Ryan to Luke and back again.

"Jesus, El, you're so hot," Ryan muttered, low and dirty.

Elliott's face set in something like determination and he came all over Ryan's stomach and chest. Ryan took in every second of it, every tiny detail that he would never normally notice, like the way his breath hitched and stalled and his muscles seemed to freeze and his eyes went wide with the sudden arch of his back. Ryan stored it all away for future reference.

As Elliott came down, his body still rocking with Luke's thrusts, occasional whimpers escaping his throat, Ryan slid his hand from Elliott's dick to Luke's hand that rested on Elliott's hip, holding on tightly to it as Luke gave a few final thrusts and cried out before everything went very quiet.

Ryan watched the two of them for a moment, the way their bodies still seemed to move together slightly as they tried to catch their breath, and then he let his hand slide down to his own dick, using everything he had seen to inspire his too-close body to just give it up, the images running vividly through his mind as his body clenched and his orgasm drowned him with a tingly pleasure from head to toe that pulsed through him over and again.

It would be easy to say that what they did wasn't a real threesome; it was certainly like no threesome Ryan had ever had before, and yet he didn't feel as sidelined as he probably should be with his role. He felt like an intrinsic part of what was happening and he felt connected to Elliott in a way he hadn't for a very long time. He thought he'd learned all there was to learn about Elliott long ago, but now, starting with his admission that he wanted two guys at once, Ryan was seeing him in a fresh light. He could never feel sidelined with a gift like that.

Half an hour later, Elliott called a cab for Luke. Ryan felt like he was being slightly rude, getting rid of him so soon after they were done, but it was comfortable as they all said goodbye with lingering kisses and friendly touches. It was understood as a one-time deal and nobody was getting shortchanged.

Elliott gave Ryan a goofy grin and then dragged him into the shower where the two of them cleaned up before opening that bottle of wine. They sat across from each other at the kitchen table, sipping wine and exchanging loved-up looks. Ryan thought those days were long gone, when they could just sit there and be in love with nothing to fill the silences.

Elliott reached across the table, brushing his fingers over the back of Ryan's hand. "Thank you."

"For what?" Ryan asked, shaking his head and taking a sip of his wine. Elliott shrugged. He looked down, his fingertips still moving over Ryan's hand.

"Getting me."

Ryan turned his hand over, holding Elliott's fingers against his palm. "It's not dirty or wrong. Definitely not the way we did it."

"No," Elliott agreed easily. He met Ryan's eyes. "I'm glad I found that out. With you. It was..." He trailed off.

Ryan smiled. "Yeah, it was. For me too," Ryan told him. Elliott smiled and maybe blushed a little bit. "You really are extraordinary, Elliott May," Ryan said fondly.

Elliott gave something close to a frown. "I don't think anybody's ever called me extraordinary before."

Ryan squeezed his fingers. "Well, sometimes people need to look a little closer."

Those words meant so much now, and he could tell that Elliott felt it too. There had been nothing wrong between them, but suddenly everything felt better than it ever had. Ryan felt closer to Elliott and their relationship felt stronger. Everything had slotted into place in the most unexpected of ways.

"Come on," Ryan said, getting to his feet and pulling Elliott with him. "Let me take you to bed."

They walked through the apartment hand in hand, turning off lights as they went, and then they lay down together in the bed they'd just shared with another man. There were no ghosts there though, no sorrows or regrets. There was just Ryan and Elliott, exactly as it should be. There was just love and happiness and security. And a very grown-up relationship.

The End

I'm Not Your Boyfriend

Lene Taylor

What does a boyfriend do?
He steps on your toes, he gets in the way, he acts like an ass. He gets jealous, he feels entitled–and then? He tells you his problems. Predictable.
From *I Wish There Was Something I Could Quit*, by Aaron Cometbus, © 2006.

Trey put down the book and sighed. Giselle, his beautiful, brown-haired, brown-eyed, brainy girlfriend, had given it to him weeks ago, saying she thought he would like it, because it was about people trying to figure out what to do with their lives. But he'd read nearly thirty pages and still didn't get it. Did she mean that boyfriend stuff was about him? And he knew what he was going to do with his life, starting on the first day of summer. He had a list:

#1. Work in the Wal-Mart warehouse and save money.
#2. Practice basketball every day.
#3. Hang out with Jordan.
#4. Get tan (but not too much–enough to show off blue eyes).
#5. Go off to college.

Working so much was going to suck, but even with his basketball scholarship in the fall, money was going to be tight once he was at the University of Albuquerque and not living with his parents anymore. Last summer had been all fun and games, working with Jordan, his best bud, and all his friends at that swanky country club, but now he was 18 and needed to act like an adult. He would work hard, and then study hard and play hard and make his parents proud.

But there was one more thing to add to the list:

#0. Break up with Giselle.

Trey had his speech ready days before the Big Event.

He and Giselle met like they usually did on Fridays, after he finished at the warehouse and she closed up the daycare center where she was working. It was hot and they decided to get ice cream; Trey thought it might help her feel better. Ice cream always put him in a better mood.

He waited till they were back in his parents' car before he got started.

"Giselle, listen, I need to tell you something." She took another lick of her strawberry ice cream and then turned to look at him. He took a deep breath. "This past year has been great, really, so great, but I think...I mean, I think maybe we shouldn't...you know...continue."

"Continue what?"

"Seeing each other. Exclusively." His ice cream was starting to melt over his hand and he quickly licked it up.

"Oh." She thought for a minute. "Why?"

"We're both working so much, it's like we hardly have time to see each other. And you said you're probably going to have to move at the end of the year. And...it just doesn't feel right anymore."

"So you want to break up now?" Trey was a little surprised at how calmly she was taking this.

"Well, I mean, I'll be away at college in September–"

"Trey, it's on the other side of town. It's not like you're moving to Alaska."

"I know, but I'll be living on campus and I have to spend most of my time with the team. I just don't think

I'll have time for a relationship."

Giselle frowned and said, "Well. I think you're being kind of a dork about this, but you do have a history of dorkiness. You got in trouble an awful lot at the country club last summer." Trey held his breath, suddenly worried that she'd found out the truth about the garden shed. "But you might actually be right. It's probably better this way."

He let out a sigh of relief. "But you'll always be special to me, you know. You were my first real girlfriend." That made her smile.

"Hey, we can still do some things together this summer, right? You're shaking your head at me. Are you serious?"

Trey reached over and put his non-sticky hand on her shoulder. "Giselle, I'm not your boyfriend anymore."

She raised an eyebrow at him. "I know, you just got done breaking up with me. But we have all the same friends. I'm not gonna stop hanging out with them just because we're not together. Are you?"

"I– I don't think I'll have time," he lied. She didn't say anything for a long minute.

"You know what? Take me home now. Please." She threw her strawberry-stained napkin in his lap. "I am so glad I didn't sleep with you."

Trey put the car in gear. Now he'd have time to see Jordan that night.

They played basketball under the lights for about an hour, not talking, just practicing, dodging, running, shooting, both of them enjoying the casual contact on the court. They finished up at 9 and then sat for a while on the pavement, sharing a big bottle of water. Trey noticed that the sweat on Jordan's skin made his caramel color glow.

"Jason and his family are away on vacation," Jordan said.

"Oh yeah?"

"So..."

"So what?" Trey was totally missing the message.

"They have a pool, remember? If we're quiet, we can go for a swim." Jordan handed the bottle back to him and smiled, shaking the sweat from the curls that hung into his eyes. He always looked like he needed a haircut.

"We're there," Trey said. "Race you to the car!"

They'd been in Jason's pool plenty of times before, but always "in public," as Jordan said. The house was at the end of a cul-de-sac and backed onto some undeveloped land, so it was easy to circle around, jump the fence, and slip into the cool water without any of the nosy neighbors spotting them. The only light was from the stars and the streetlights and everything was washed in shades of blue and grey.

Trey slid underwater and swam slowly across the length of the pool. He came up right behind Jordan, who had his eyes closed as he floated near the steps. "Hi," Trey whispered, and bit Jordan's lovely earlobe, gently but insistently.

"Hi," Jordan whispered back. "And don't stop." Trey wrapped his arms around his waist and pulled him close; the water had cooled his own hard-on–which made its appearance the moment they'd silently stripped off their clothes–but now the warmth of their bodies brought it back full-force, and he slowly pushed it against the small of Jordan's smooth, hard back. Trey made a mental list of all the places they'd done it, just so he could add this to the list: the shed, the car, the parking lot of In-N-Out Burger, Jordan's bedroom, the bathroom of the mall, the kitchen of the country club–

Jordan moved Trey's hands down to his cock; Trey was only too happy to stroke him the way he liked it, with a firm grip and long smooth motions that ended in a little ball-squeeze at the end. Jordan leaned back into him and Trey kissed the back of his neck over and over, loving the taste of him, the smell of him, the feel of his slick wet skin on his lips. With a swirl of water, Jordan spun around and opened his mouth wide to Trey, and they kissed for long minutes, with only the sound of faraway cars and the wind from the mountains in their ears.

"Come up here," Jordan said, pulling Trey onto the steps so they were mostly out of the water. "We need some natural lube." He spit into his hand and sat facing Trey, then pressed their erections together and started urgently stroking them both. "Like this, Trey, like this," he panted, soft brown eyes glowing.

Trey added his own hand to the mix and soon they were both slick with pre-come, wet skin shining in the starlight, warm and pulsing in the hot air; Jordan thrust against him faster, harder, and with a small strangled sigh he came straight up in the air, on his chest, on Trey's arm, and the look on his face, lost in orgasm, was enough to push Trey to the edge, filling Jordan's hand as he shook and jerked. They were hot, and sticky, and Trey had never been happier.

Jordan kissed him and nibbled on his lower lip. "Think we should tell Jason he needs to get his pool cleaned?"

Trey laughed softly. "Nah. I'm sure we're not the first...or the last." He licked a drop of the white stuff off his arm, then sank back down in the water. Jordan followed him and they swam slowly into the deep end. "Hey, I did something important today."

"Yeah? What up?"

"I called it off. With her."

"You did what?" Jordan snapped fiercely.

"I broke up with Giselle. I thought you'd be happy about that..." Trey trailed off.

"Trey, man, are you stupid or what? Don't answer that. You couldn't stick with her just until the end of summer?" Jordan pushed Trey away roughly. "What were you thinking?"

"I was thinking that now we could spend the summer together! Isn't that what you want?" He floated closer but Jordan was having none of it.

"Trey. Giselle was the only reason you and I could be together in the first place! Do you not get that? Do you want everyone to find out about us?" He realized he was getting loud and dropped his voice to a whisper again. "Remember the shed last year?"

Trey surely did remember the shed. It was the one place at the country club that both he and Jordan could legitimately disappear to, and they spent as much time as possible getting busy behind the golf carts and rakes. Once they'd almost been caught by Bryan, the son of the club's owners; somehow they convinced him they were looking for new hoops for the croquet set, and swore to each other they'd never do it again. That promise lasted about six hours.

"No one will know. And what if they do? What's the worst thing that could happen?"

"I don't want to get my ass kicked on a daily basis. Like it wasn't bad enough being one of the only black kids in East High! I am not gonna be the queer black kid at community college. That's what's gonna happen, Trey."

"But–but–"

"Listen. You and me–it's not cool. You, you're gonna go off to college at a real school–yeah, it might be just across town but it's another world. You got your scholarship, you got your basketball team, you got it all. And I got to stay here and work and go to a crappy school until I can get out of here. You ever think about that?" Trey didn't answer.

"Look, we can be friends and all," Jordan said, coming closer again.

Trey was confused and scared and hurt and angry all at once. He'd never stopped to think about what they did, or what it meant; it just felt right to be with Jordan and not with Giselle and maybe it was time he used the word. For himself.

"I guess...I guess I'm the queer kid with the

basketball scholarship, then." Jordan snorted with a suppressed laugh. "But don't you want to be with me anymore?"

"Trey, I'm not your boyfriend."

He and Jordan played basketball on Friday nights (and even hooked up twice more–Jordan said they needed to "get it out of their systems") but they stopped hanging out all the time like they used to. He tried to do some fun stuff with Giselle and their formerly mutual friends, but he got the distinct feeling he wasn't really welcome anymore, and he soon gave that up too. So he worked, and practiced shooting hoops alone, and wondered if he was getting too tan. Warehouse work slacked off, though, so he started to look around for something else to do. He'd heard they were still taking on extra staff at the country club and made an appointment to see the summer hiring manager.

Which turned out to be Bryan. He sat behind the big wooden desk, looking immaculate, as usual; today he was wearing a bright pink shirt, white pants, and a black jacket that, along with the amount of product in his white-blond hair, made him look like an ad for a very expensive ice cream shop.

"Well! What can I do for you, Trey?" He smiled warmly. After the fighting and fireworks last summer, Bryan had proved to everyone that he wasn't just a spoiled rich brat like his sister, and that he could be a nice guy if he chose to. Also that he could kick ass at baseball. He and Trey and Jordan hadn't become friends, exactly; just friend-ly.

"Hey. I didn't know you were in management now. I was looking for some hours if you've got 'em."

"Sure, we can always use more help. You can caddy if you promise not to drive the carts into the pool."

"Very funny. Not. I'll take as much time as you've got– I'm gonna need the money for college." Bryan had light blue eyes. Why hadn't he ever noticed that before?

"Right, you got into U of A on that scholarship. Congrats. I'm going to New York in September. I got into Parsons. Can't wait to hit the Big Apple." Trey wondered what kind of school Parsons was but thought it would make him look stupider than he already felt. Even though they'd been in school together for four years, Bryan always made him feel like he was a hick from the country.

"What about your sister?" Ivana, Bryan's horrible twin sister, was universally hated by everyone at the country club, including Bryan.

"I think my parents are sending her to Europe or something. Maybe she'll find a brain while she's there. What's up with Giselle?" Bryan shoved some papers toward him and stood up.

"Oh, I don't really know...we broke up and I haven't seen her much lately," Trey mumbled as he started to fill in his name.

"Sorry," Bryan said, but he really didn't sound sorry at all.

Working two jobs wasn't bad and the money was great. It was even kind of fun to be back at the country club; he already knew where everything was, and Bryan seemed to go out of his way to get him perks like new uniforms and caddy jobs with big tippers. Sometimes they even ate together in the kitchen.

"So what do you do for fun these days?" Bryan asked, while they finished off the shrimp scampi from that day's lunch.

"Not much. Practice b-ball. That's about it."

"You want to come to my house to watch a movie sometime? I mean, I'm here so much I don't get to have much fun either. My house is nuts. You'll love it."

"Um, sure, yeah, that would be cool," Trey said, trying to hide his surprise behind a mouthful of shrimp.

"Great. You can bring Jordan if he wants to come..."

"I–I don't hang out with him much anymore. Too

busy," Trey lied.

"Oh. OK," Bryan said. "Listen, gotta get back to work–how about tomorrow night?" Trey nodded. He wondered why Bryan was grinning as he left the room.

The house did not disappoint. It was huge and empty and cool, and their footsteps echoed on the marble floors and up the stairs. Expensive stuff everywhere, lots of rooms and doors and hallways that seemed to lead off into other houses. "Isn't there anyone here?" Trey asked. It felt like a museum, not a home.

"Mom and Dad are out for the night, some political party thing. Ivana is in LA. The housekeeper is probably in the kitchen, getting things ready for tomorrow. You want something to eat or drink?" Bryan led them into a big room with shiny things in it; the lights came up automatically as they entered and Trey could see a huge plasma TV, stereo, game system–gadget paradise.

"Wow. Is this the, like, home entertainment center?" Trey asked, amazed.

"It's my entertainment center. It's also my room," he said, and pointed to the corner. Somehow Trey had missed the huge bed, covered with pillows. He hoped he didn't look as envious as he felt.

"Wow," Trey repeated. He sank down into one of the beanbag chairs in front of the TV and looked around for the remote. Bryan hung up his jacket and stood silently for a minute, looking at the floor. Then he came over and sat on the floor next to Trey. This close, he could smell Bryan's expensive cologne. He smelled good.

"Trey, listen," Bryan said, and put his hand on Trey's arm. "Last summer...I knew about you and Jordan. Wait!" he said, as Trey started to get up, panicking. "Don't freak out. Come on, Trey, it's me. I'm about as gay as they come. So to speak. I saw you guys in the shed and after that it was easy to see how much you were into each other." Trey felt a rush of relief on top of the fear: relief that someone else finally knew the truth, but why was Bryan telling him this now? Was this some new scheme of Ivana's? He tried to slow his breathing. He couldn't stop his heart from pounding. And suddenly he was aware of his growing hard-on.

"It's not last summer anymore," Trey said. He didn't move as Bryan's hand slipped down to his knee.

"I know," Bryan said. "I thought I'd gotten over my crush on you, but apparently that's not the case." He moved closer till his lips were an inch away from Trey's. "We don't have to watch a movie," he whispered.

"No, we don't," Trey said, and leaned over and kissed Bryan hard.

It didn't take long for them to move things over to the bed, where Bryan pushed Trey down onto the pillows, stripped him, and kissed him from his head to his toes, wearing his infectious grin all the time. He paused for a moment to whip off his shirt and pants (No underwear! Is that a rich people thing? Trey wondered.) and then laid down on top of Trey and sucked on his lower lip. "I have wanted to do this for so long," he said. "And it's better than I ever thought it would be."

Trey was too overwhelmed to do anything but kiss him back. Bryan's hard-on–bigger than Jordan's–was pressed hard against his own, so he started to rock his hips a little as he ran his hands down Bryan's smooth back. When both of them stopped to breathe, Trey asked, "Do you want me to–"

"Just leave it to me," Bryan said, still grinning. Then he kissed his way down to Trey's cock and licked and sucked and caressed and swirled his tongue seven different ways until Trey thought he would pass out. And then Bryan pushed his legs up and worked his tongue into his ass and Trey figured he'd died and gone to heaven.

He felt Bryan's finger slide into him and moaned in response; soon it was two fingers and Bryan's lips were wrapped around his cock again. He could feel his orgasm building, closer and closer–

Bryan stopped everything he was doing. "Don't come yet, Trey, not yet, not yet..." he said, and kissed Trey deeply. A few more moments and he had a condom and lube and eased himself into Trey's tight ass until he couldn't go any deeper. Trey was desperate for release.

"Now, please, now," he moaned, clutching the pillows and lifting his hips.

"Right now," Bryan said, and fucked him hard and fast and with expert skill, and thirty seconds later Trey came hard and fast into Bryan's hand and all over his chest, lights exploding behind his eyes, waves of heat flowing over him. A few more thrusts and Bryan came too; Trey could feel his cock pulsing inside. Bryan collapsed on top of him, panting. "Good?"

"Wow," Trey said.

That was the first week of July. For the rest of the month and through August, Trey went to Bryan's house to "watch a movie" twice a week and get fucked within an inch of his life. Bryan had vastly more experience than Trey and was only too happy to pass along the knowledge of toys, porn, positions, lubes, and Jell-o. It didn't come naturally, but Trey learned how to be a good top–you just had to work hard and practice, practice, practice.

Summer was almost over and it was insanely hot. Trey was happy to spend as much time in Bryan's air-conditioned palace as he could, before they both had to go their separate ways. He hadn't seen Giselle in weeks and didn't care; hadn't seen Jordan in weeks and still cared a little; wasn't sure at all how he felt about Bryan. They'd done everything possible to each other in Bryan's bedroom, but Trey still didn't feel a real emotional connection. He was always happy to see Bryan, and never sorry to say goodbye. And that was it. And soon they wouldn't see each other for months. Did that mean they were breaking up?

Late one night, after they'd finished a very sweaty session with the double-ended dildo (that vibrated!),

Trey decided to say it.

"You're leaving soon, huh?" he asked, licking some come off Bryan's hand. He wasn't sure whose it was and it didn't matter.

"Yeah. Mom and Dad sent most of my stuff out to New York already. I get their big apartment all to myself. You should come out there sometime. It'll be fun." Bryan had his eyes closed and wore the ever-present grin.

"About that...I'm not– I mean, I never thought we'd stay– you know..." The words kept falling out of his mouth but didn't get any closer to what he meant.

"Boyfriends? You're great, Trey, but I didn't think you were my boyfriend. There's a great word: fuck-buddy. That's more like it. I don't even know if I'm ready for a real boyfriend." He sat up and kissed Trey. "You weren't gonna propose to me, were you?"

Trey laughed in relief. "Friends. And fuck-buddies." Somehow that word made him hard again, so he put Bryan's hand on his cock to show him that everything was cool.

"And if we're both home at Christmas, maybe we can hook up again. Who knows what kinds of toys they have in New York?" Bryan's hot mouth covered Trey's and they broke open the box of glow-in-the-dark condoms.

College was just as hard as Trey had thought it would be: basketball practice twice a day, classes the rest of time, and for the first few weeks hardly enough energy to read and get his homework done. But eventually he got used to it and started enjoying being away from his parents and flaunting his status on the Red Hawks.

And there was Brett, the cute boy in his Poli Sci class who asked him to have coffee, and then asked him on a date, and then asked him for a kiss when they said goodnight. Brett didn't really follow sports, but he was willing to listen to Trey talk about the perfect layup; Trey was happy to listen to Brett tell stories about how important it was to have a third political party in the U.S. Their dates were normal dinner-and-a-movie affairs and even after a few weeks they hadn't done more than make out a little. Trey decided to make the first move.

They had gotten a late dinner of very fine chile verde and were walking back towards campus. Holding hands. Trey went through his mental list of preparations:

#1. No practice tomorrow morning
#2. Roommate gone for the weekend
#3. Clean sheets on the bed
#4. Lube and condoms (normal ones) in bedside table

They had just come to the point where they usually said goodnight when Brett suddenly reached over and kissed him. This was definitely the night to make a move.

"Can I go back to your room with you?" Brett said softly, their lips still touching. "I know we've been taking it slow, but I just can't wait anymore. Is that OK? We don't have to do everything if you don't want to..."

"Everything. With you. That's what I want," Trey said, wrapping Brett in his arms. Brett's erection pressing against his leg almost made him come in his pants. Brett pulled back and gazed at him, eyes shining in the moonlight.

"Trey, I like you so much. I want to be your boyfriend."

"Really?" Trey felt Bryan's grin spreading across his face.

"Really." And then they kissed and went back to Trey's room and fucked four times that night, and lived happily ever after till the end of their second year in college, when, like all college couples, they broke up. But it was a wonderful two years.

The End

When George MacFadden was Eaten by a Dragon

Colleen Wylie

When George MacFadden was eaten by a dragon, the unforeseen tragedy caused his boyfriend some problems.

Chief among these was the press coverage. The task of shaping Fleet Street's initial, inchoate views of the event fell, naturally enough, to Charles Newman. He wasn't an image consultant, exactly, but anyone with an image problem, and access to Charlie, would naturally begin right there. He occasionally referred difficult cases to carefully chosen specialists, but only if they involved failures of personal hygiene, politics or women, all of which he considered indefensible.

"Tom, Tom, Tom," Charlie said, when Thomas Grisewood's personal secretary/housekeeper admitted him to the sunny first floor drawing room.

Until yesterday, George and his partner had lived quietly here, collecting watercolors, sharing fine wines, and playing some serious chess. Charlie glanced around with sharp eyes, making valuations of recent acquisitions and assessing opening gambits stalled without prospect of resolution. After a moment, he threw himself into an armchair and crossed his cranefly legs. "Tom." He frowned down his chiseled nose. "Tom."

"Is that all you're going to say?" Thomas protested.

"You really have fucked up this time."

"I...What the hell are you talking about?"

"I hate to say this, Tom. People pay attention to you. It's not that you're clever, or amusing, or even as good looking as you used to be, but you are...well, people aren't frightened by you. You're gay but you're not promiscuous, embarrassing or inclined to musical theatre. You're presentable, acceptable and even decorative." He paused and fingered the petals of the white hydrangeas that filled a green glass vase by his chair, noticing that it exactly resembled one of the new paintings. "You used to be decorative."

"But I'm still here," Thomas exclaimed. "I'm not going anywhere. I'm not the one who...who...How can you be so...I thought at least I could expect some sympathy from..."

"I am very sympathetic. I won't pretend I liked George, but...well, let's just say that although I disliked George..."

"I. Loved. Him."

"So you've said."

"I did."

"But now we know you didn't."

"What?" Thomas, who had been curled, like a convalescent, on the day bed in the window, leapt to his feet and gesticulated at nothing in particular. "I didn't love him? Because...because what? Because I wasn't there? When a dragon dropped out of a cloudless blue sky, sank its claws into him and flew off? Because I'm not chasing after it even though no one seems to know where it went? In what sense is that not loving him? Or not loving him enough? Or not walking about with an automatic weapon just in case..." He folded back onto the day bed, overcome at his own inadequacy. "Like I'd have hit it if I did have a gun."

"Spare me the tears," Charlie said.

Thomas defiantly knocked away a drop of liquid from his cheek. "If I had hit it, it would have dropped him."

"That's true. Have you seen the *Express*?"

"What?" With an effort, Thomas stopped imagining George McFadden lying, like carrion, on the street. "No. I haven't been outside. There are photographers.

And I don't read the *Express* anyway. Why the hell would I suddenly start reading the *Express*?"

"And you haven't answered the phone."

"No."

"Or looked at your emails."

"No."

"Or chosen the flowers for the funeral."

Thomas opened a denying mouth and closed it again. Charlie had the grace to place a hand discretely in front of his smile.

"So what bullshit are they pushing? Dragging up all the old lies about me and Vladimir at Oxford?"

"That was what I expected."

"I don't care. I stopped caring years ago. The world needs to get over it. I'm gay, I'm successful, I'm—"

"Oh, stop it. You're not the only one who stopped caring. Your sex life was yesterday's news, until yesterday."

"And I used to be happy, before my boyfriend was eaten by a dragon."

Charlie contemplated the man he'd come, out of finely calculated utilitarian instincts, to advise. The sun was making playful haloes in the soft waves of Thomas's hair, hair the golden shade of perfectly toasted white bread. Naturally silver-grey eyes had momentarily picked up a hint of sapphire from the sky. Cerulean, Charlie thought. It was the kind of word he normally scorned, but he almost felt inspired to say it aloud. Cerulean. A word like a caress. He discarded it. "What you've overlooked, Tom, is that dragons are notoriously choosy in their eating habits."

The eyes lost that stolen blueness as they narrowed. "What?"

"Virgins, Tom. Dragons eat virgins. Every schoolchild in London knows that dragons feast on the innocent, the pure. The intact." Charlie's teeth were very white as his tongue clicked out the staccato consonants.

"But..."

"Our good friends at the *Express* are not scandalized by your homosexuality, or not today at any rate. They are outraged by your deceit. They have been taken for a ride, and they are not amused. You have set yourself up as a minority, a reject, an angel on the way out from heaven, misunderstood, (yet understanding), the acceptable darling of the only-just-liberal middle classes. Along the way, you've seduced their wives (metaphorically), won over their sisters and distracted their mistresses. You've even, and don't deny it, because I've seen you, you've even had the pansy cheek to turn your charm on their mothers. And you're not even bloody queer."

"But..."

"You can't argue with the facts, Tom. Dragons only eat virgins. A dragon ate George. Therefore George was a virgin. Therefore you have not had carnal knowledge of the pretty, but vacuous, young fool. Therefore you are not, or not in any way that matters to a world obsessed with the flesh, homosexual. QED. In short, you're a fraud."

"But..."

"Aren't you going to offer me a cup of tea?"

Thomas was momentarily lost for words. By the time he'd ordered tea and checked whether his guest would prefer Victoria sponge or tarte citronne, his outrage had abated enough for him to strike a resolute pose in front of the hearth and defend himself.

"George is not a...a virgin."

"It's not what I'm saying, Tom. It's what the press is saying."

"And why the fuck would I pretend to be gay if I wasn't? It's not a VIP pass to anywhere, even now. Gay men still get glassed in the pubs round here on Saturday nights." Thomas paused for a reaction, but Charlie knew his rhetorical tricks too well, having taught him most of them, to be startled by a few words designed to demonstrate that Thomas Grisewood did not, as one might imagine, live in the nineteenth century.

"These little tarts are splendid."

Thomas glared at him. "If anyone's making a career out of an ersatz queer aesthetic..."

Charlie tickled up a crumb of wonderfully short pie crust onto the tip of his index finger and wrapped his tongue round it thoughtfully. "Pubs round here? Really? How fascinating. I'm here to help, Tom. But as you yourself have said, I do my best work when I believe the shit I'm peddling."

"I am not lying!"

His visitor sighed and eyed the remaining tarts with regret before putting aside his plate. "You played chess with Louisa last night."

"So now I'm pretending to be gay so I can steal my friend's wives."

"I wouldn't put it past you. Or maybe you're just impotent. We could put that in the water and see if it floats."

Thomas's natural good manners obliged him to close the doors into the drawing room before he relieved Charlie of his teacup and knelt astride his lap. "Are you hoping for a demonstration?" he demanded.

Charlie shook his head and gave a token wriggle of protest. "I was only going to suggest we try and prise Vladimir out of that bogus Orthodox retreat he's running and see if he'll do Jonathan Ross. Or one of those other crappy Friday night talk shows everyone says they haven't watched. From what I remember, he'll lie pretty convincingly about having sex with you in exchange for a chance to sound off about the meaning of life on a terrestrial channel."

"Why are you always so rude about my boyfriends?" Thomas sounded petulant, but his hands were busy with shirt buttons.

Charlie shrugged. "You need to ask?"

"George has been eaten by a dragon."

"We don't really know that. It seems likely, but..."

Thomas pulled the front of Charlie's shirt clear of his waistband rather roughly, sending one of the buttons spinning across the carpet...

"Careful!"

...and ran a firm finger down the center of Charlie's chest to just above his navel.

"You're just going through the motions, Tom. Just..."

Thomas leaned forward to silence him with a kiss.

Charlie pursed his lips and wriggled again. "You're heavier than you think you are," he complained when Thomas paused for breath.

"Charlie!"

"I get paid to lie to the public, not to my clien–"

"I don't pay you!"

"Well I hope you'll reconsider that, because you really need me now."

As if confirming this, Tom laced his fingers into Charlie' hair and pulled him into another kiss. After a moment, Charlie let his lips fall open.

Thomas immediately froze. He sat back on his heels. "I'm sorry. I don't know what came over me."

"Fear that your career is about to go down the pan."

When Thomas began to push himself off Charlie's lap, his visitor pressed his thighs against the arms of the chair, trapping Thomas's knees.

"Now hold on a moment, Tom. You are being entirely ridiculous, as always, but you need to think about someone other than yourself for once. If George wasn't a virgin, and frankly, nothing about the way he behaved has ever given me any reason to suppose he was, then we need to make that perfectly clear to people. We are all at risk. Well, more of us are at risk. Some people of course are no longer at risk, but virgins are a smaller group and mostly quite safe in their nurseries and schoolrooms. It's the sluts we have to worry about. You have to worry about. You have to make sure that everyone understands that being a slut is no defense. I'm sorry to say this, but it's your duty.

What we need are some particularly memorable, and preferably very visual–because we have to make sure that people go away with the after image engraved on their eyeballs–some very memorable accounts of exactly how slutty George McFadden was. He's got a bit of the choirboy about him. We can't let people think, 'Oh, maybe he was a virgin. Maybe dragons haven't changed the eating habits of the last two millennia,' and the next thing they know, they're sandwiched between two slices of whatever passes for bread among dragons, slathered in hot chili sauce. What do you think? Do any particular incidents spring to mind? Involving the two of you? I think this has to be a firsthand soundbite. The public is depending on you."

"You want me to tell you...?"

"There's no point me paying to fly Vladimir over if you're going to be utterly unconvincing, Tom. No point at all. And I've always thought you come over as rather...well, undersexed."

Thomas attempted to push down on the chair's firmly upholstered arms and extricate both knees at once. This was no more successful than his earlier one-sided efforts.

He gave up and slammed his weight down hard onto Charlie's thighs.

The taller man sucked in a breath as the keys in Thomas's back pocket cut into his flesh. He wriggled to soothe the abused muscle on the lining of his suit trousers.

"It's absolutely imperative that you're as convincing as you can be. Maybe we should run through whatever coupling you're going to talk about, so you don't get confused over the details."

"A dry run?" Thomas demanded sarcastically.

"Oh, yes, of course a dry run. Absolutely." The wriggle was frankly suggestive now. "And with detail. Detail is very convincing. And it has to be something ordinary people can identify with, not too outrageous. Fisting, to pick an example at random, might be a step too far, but it has to be actual sex, as most of us understand it. I love that story about George bringing you to a shuddering climax on the metro platform at Musée d'Orsay, but I've heard he didn't even touch you, so it doesn't really count."

Thomas was momentarily speechless. "Who told you about that?"

"Who do you think?"

"George." Thomas smiled indulgently, like a parent whose marital secrets have been babbled to the world by his infant son and heir. "I do love him."

"Did. You did love him."

"Yes, all right! I did love him! You don't have to go on about it. I didn't put everything into the past tense when Alastair ran off with a Polish builder."

"Architect."

"Bricklayer."

"Well, no, you didn't. You were...you were supportive. I'm sorry."

"Yes, I was." Thomas surprised Charlie by emitting a little hiccough of suppressed laughter. "You just wouldn't get off the phone."

"I needed to talk to someone."

"That was the night George and I..."

"I know. The night you met. You've told me. I almost ruined it, you've told..."

Thomas was actually giggling now.

"Why's that so funny?"

"Yes, I was very good to you. I'd just met someone really special, we'd had two bottles of champagne, I'd invited him back here, I'd turned off my mobile because someone kept ringing. I didn't even look to see who it was. Then when we walked in here, I picked up the house phone out of habit, you told me what had happened, and I actually asked George to go. You really should be grateful."

"You've told me this before." Charlie paused, not sure where this was going. "And I know I probably said I was sorry he ever came back, and I know that might seem a little callous, in the circumstances, but I didn't know he was going to be eaten by a dragon."

"Do you want to know what happened next?"

"Probably not."

"I'll tell you anyway."

"Oh. I see. Now you're going to tell me that the whole time you were being wise and world-weary and 'it'll get better in time blah-blah-blah' you were thinking about *him*."

"I was waaaaay beyond thinking."

"You weren't bloody masturbating were you?"

"No."

"Thank heaven for that."

"George didn't go."

"He stayed? He waited? We must have been talking for at least an hour. Don't tell me he picked up another handset and bloody listened!"

"No, he..."

"I'll kill him. I mean, I'll...I'll kill you." Charlie wrapped his long fingers round Thomas's neck and applied a pressure that wasn't entirely playful.

Thomas thrust his hand, not entirely playfully, between Charlie's legs. Once Charlie released him and the blood stopped hammering in his ears, he continued his narrative, but absentmindedly failed to remove his hand. "He closed the door. I was concentrating on you, and I thought he'd gone. Then I heard him moving in the room. I was sitting in this chair..." Thomas gestured at the handset on the highly polished table beside them to establish the plausibility of his account. "I'd sat down without thinking. I didn't even think about showing George out. I was surprised, and quite upset. Alastair was good for you. He drew the curtains...George, I mean, not Alastair..."

"Alastair was here too?"

"No, Alastair was in Bucharest with Gerik. Remember?"

"Yes, strangely, all the events of that appalling day are clearly imprinted on my memory. I was being sarcastic."

"He drew the curtains, and I watched him, while you were telling me about the row you'd had in the taxi. He has the most amazing hands. Have you noticed? His fingers are very long. Almost as long as yours. And he has the most perfect nails."

"He has a very good manicurist."

"No. He takes care of his hands, of course, he has to. But he has naturally beautiful nails. He never bites them..." Thomas pulled his hand free to look, sadly, at the evidence that he had less self control. Charlie grunted frustratedly, grabbed the hand and thrust it back where it had been. "...and they don't ever break, or get ragged, or all ridged. He has...he had beautiful nails."

"He has/had a very good manicurist, she's called Mrs. Gilly, and I'll introduce you to her if you like, because she doesn't take clients in off the street, and if you're wondering how George managed to get on her list, it was because he and her son were, shall we say, best friends. That and he's never washed a dish in his life. I'm surprised he's never told you about Mrs. Gilly, but perhaps he finds your chewed extremities embarrassing."

"I thought you wanted to know about me and George."

"I've changed my mind. The idea that he was sucking you off while I was pouring out my deepest, most wounded..."

"He wasn't. He didn't touch me. He drew the curtains and turned the lights off. And then he undressed."

"In the dark?"

"Yes."

"How do you know?"

"What do you mean, how do I know? He told me what he was doing...or...not quite that. He told me what he was feeling, what he was wanting, what he was...what every part of his body was feeling about every part of mine. What he was imagining. How his skin was chafing to be free of anything that kept it away from mine. How his clothes were like a straightjacket, how confined he felt. How..."

"How long did it take him to get you off?"

"That wasn't the point. It was all new, he was exploring me, discovering me, adoring me, charming me, exhorting me."

"Fascinating. He said at the Musée, it took him twenty minutes. Did he get quicker with practice, or slower? How long?"

"Every breath, every heart beat, the faintest pulse in the smallest vein in my..."

"Cock?"

"Oh, shit, Charles." Thomas looked rather lost. "Would it hurt you to let me remember?"

"I'm going out later. I don't want to have to change my suit."

"Well," Thomas said apologetically, edging backwards a little on Charlie's lap, "you wanted a blow by blow account."

"Yes, yes, yes, action, conflict, resolution. No one's going to listen to all this talk."

"And anyway, it took exactly as long as it took you to get from the row in the taxi to the bottle of champagne in the petrol tank of your Ferrari."

Charlie took a moment to assess this. "Oh. Oh! Right. You know, I wondered at the time, but I thought you were really upset about the car."

"Not that upset, Charlie. I could be upset about the champagne, if that would help."

"It's a bit late now. I'm over the car anyway. So, George did his gay chatline act, and when you finally managed to slam the phone down on my broken heart, my tedious histrionics, he was sitting there stark naked?"

"No. He must have got dressed again. Or maybe he never actually undressed. To be honest, Charlie, I've never seen George in a state of undress. I've never needed to."

"You've...he's been...never?"

A sudden shriek from elsewhere in the apartment interrupted them. There were a few moments of complete silence as the personal secretary/housekeeper rushed up the solidly built and deeply carpeted stairs, then the door was flung open.

"...George," she mouthed, too overcome to actually speak. "...coming home."

Thomas had already scrambled off Charlie's lap and turned his back to the door before she arrived, but Charlie was calmly refastening his surviving buttons in full view. "What a pity," he said.

The personal secretary/housekeeper glared at him and left.

"Well, I'm pleased for you," Charlie said, tucking one half of his shirt tails into his trousers. "Bereavement is so disruptive."

There was a sudden crescendo of noise from outside the window, then the front door opened and almost immediately slammed shut. The squeals and exclamations of a joyful reunion spilled into the room.

"You know those two are..." Charlie began, then stopped. There was something about Thomas's face that forbade sarcasm, or even frankness.

"He's home," Thomas said softly. "He's home." He frowned at Charlie. "So, Charles, what potentially disastrous pronouncements are you going to make about our relationship, or lack of it?"

"Well, I don't know. I'm not sure. I don't want you to come across as slightly pathetic. Let's try another angle. Has George ever claimed to have royal blood, do you know? Either side of the blanket? Was there some rumored liaison a couple of generations back between a minor prince and a half-wit scullery maid with a walleye and a clubfoot? Might a dragon have got hold of the wrong idea?"

"Hi, Charlie," George said, pausing in the doorway

with one arm draped up the frame and the other draped down the leading edge of the half open door, so that his admittedly perfect nails were fully on display. A small cut in his lovely ivory brow was crisscrossed with steri-strip above a half closed eye at the center of a red-purple bruise. His shirt was open to his waist. "Who's got hold of the wrong idea?"

Thomas moved towards him. "George," he said, and stopped short, just out of reach.

"Tom," George said. "Tom." He beamed. "I escaped. I bribed it with..." He paused.

"Do go on," Charlie said. "You know you can rely on my discretion."

George shook his head. "I don't think I can."

"The small amount of cocaine, for personal use only, that you happened to be carrying?" Charlie suggested. "Tom's credit card?"

"Oh, you know. All that, but mostly shiny stuff. Cufflinks, shirt studs, newish pennies. It didn't seem to be very bright. I had to give it my new iPhone, and that's such a waste, because it can't use it, not with those talons." He suddenly took the step that closed the space between them, and seized Thomas's hands in his. "I'll never complain about you biting your nails again, Tom. Talons are such a turn off."

"Really," Thomas said, in rather a tight voice.

"I love your nails. Your lovely, gentle, nibbled nails." George bent his head and drew the tips of Thomas's fingers into his mouth.

"Charlie, I think you said you were leaving." Tom had closed his eyes.

"Are you asking me to go, Tom?"

"It was very kind of you to come and keep me company, but I'm absolutely fine now."

George was backing towards a chair, and drawing Thomas with him.

"My pleasure. In the unlikely event of a repeat occurrence, you know where to find me."

"I do, yes."

George sat and pulled Thomas down to straddle his lap.

"I'll tell the press you won't be leaving the building any time soon."

George looked up. He noticed that Charlie's shirt was misbuttoned and untucked. He opened his mouth to comment. Thomas picked up a lemon tart and pushed it, entire, between George's lips.

"No talking," he said. "Absolutely no more talking."

The End

You Know You Should be a Better Person (But You're Not)

Karmen Ghia

With apologies to Jay McInerney (or maybe he should thank me).

You know you're unlucky when you and Thad G get to the post office after it's closed. You knock politely on the glass door and are ignored. Thad G slams your body against the glass door until a postal employee threatens to call the police. You know it could be worse, but you're not sure how.

"I swear, Thad, the money is there," you whine like the sniveling little creep you are. "They open at 8:30 tomorrow, I'll meet you–"

"I'm not meeting you anywhere," Thad says in a way that makes your flesh crawl, as you marvel yet again that he can drag you down the street twisting your arm, while lighting a cigarette and talk at the same time. You hope he isn't going to kill you now, but it's hard to know what Thad G might do depending on his mood. He has a reputation for being a very moody guy.

You know cocaine is bad for you, you know running up a bill with Thad's employer is also bad for you. You know lying to your big sister–the only person in your whole family who will still speak to you–is bad. You know she sent you that money order to pay the people who let you sleep on their floor with their pit bull, and won't give you your stuff until you pay them. You also know they will never see any of that money because you're going to cash your sister's money order and give it to Thad G and hope he doesn't beat you up too much to cover the interest your coke dealer wants and knows he's not going to get.

You know you should be a better person, but you're not. As Thad G drags you down the street to his beat-up Chevy Impala, you wish you'd thought of this before. You also wish you'd left town last week when you knew something challenging was going to happen to you this week. You wish you could predict the future and act appropriately on it. You wish Thad G's car had a passenger door handle on the inside of the car. You know this doesn't matter because you'd never have the guts to jump out of a moving vehicle. You also know you wouldn't get very far if you did because Thad G has handcuffed your right hand to your left ankle. You wish you didn't feel so stupid, although that's a moot point by now, but you might be too stupid to realize that. You keep quiet because you know enough not to provoke him. You look out the window, you don't ask where he's taking you. You will know soon enough.

He parks in front of a grim apartment building with dead grass and broken toys in front of it. He uncuffs you and drags you across the driver's seat to get out of the car, which he does not lock because everyone knows this is Thad G's car and dying for fucking with it would be painful, pointless and humiliating. Anyone with any brains would steal a newer car from someone less lethal than Thad G.

Going into the building, you notice what you think is his name on the buzzer panel: Thaddeus Gorski. Even this name that might be his name intimidates you, but you're not sure why. You are shoved up three flights of broken, filthy stairs to his apartment. It has the most boring furniture you have ever seen and looks like no one lives there.

"Find shit to clean this place with," he says, throwing himself on the couch where he can see you rummaging under the sink and in the bathroom until you find a broom, rags and Comet powder.

You get to work. You're glad he doesn't have a dog. You hate cleaning up after dogs. You wash a lot of dishes without breaking any and have to really scrub the stove, twice. The bathroom is something you hope you can forget very soon. After you sweep the floors, you dilute some vinegar in hot water to wash them with because there isn't any ammonia or bleach in the place. There's a laundry basket full of bunched-up sheets and towels in the bedroom. Thad tells you to make the bed, which only has some naked pillows and tangled blankets up on it. You find lube and used condoms in the bed. You also find one very high heeled shoe there. You never find the other one. But you're good at making beds, hospital corners and all, so it looks nice when you're done.

Thad comes into the bedroom. He looks at the bed, the high heel on the window sill, and then at you. He tells you to wash your hands. Then he takes you down to the car again. Maybe he's going to kill you now that he has a clean apartment. Maybe you shouldn't have done such a good job.

He takes you to the grocery store and makes you push the basket while he throws food in it. Ham, eggs, bacon, rice, cheese, milk, beer, more beer, wheat bread, instant coffee, whole milk, potato chips, mushrooms, an onion, celery, kielbasa, regular butter, and peanut butter. He also buys ammonia, toilet paper, paper towels, liquid soap, shampoo, a toothbrush, lube and condoms. He took all the money you had on you, which wasn't much, when he grabbed you. You assume that's partly what he used to pay for the groceries and stuff.

Back in his apartment, he tells you to wash your hands and start cooking.

"What? Cook what?" you whine like the pathetic jerk you are.

"Figure it out," he says. He takes a warm beer and pops the bottle cap off with his bare hands. Flopping back onto the couch, he looks as mean as ever. Possibly he looks meaner because he looks hungry, too.

You are, for you, lucky this time. In one of the few jobs you managed not to get fired from in the first week, you learned to cook a little when you weren't waiting tables. You look at the groceries, you look in cupboards. You find very little in the cupboards, but you do find salt and pepper. You fry half the bacon in the frying pan while you cut up the mushrooms, onion and a quarter of the kielbasa. Thad comes in and eats half the bacon off the paper towels you were blotting the grease off on while you're sautéing the vegetables and kielbasa in the bacon grease. You say nothing, but you eat some bacon yourself when he leaves. You scoop the meat and vegetables out of the grease and onto paper towels to drain. You get a sauce pan really hot and dump six eggs and butter into it and, while broiling some bread, scramble the eggs very quickly. You put a piece of toast on a plate, pile the vegetables, kielbasa and bacon on them, and then pile the eggs on top of that. You arrange squares of toast around this to keep it from spilling out the sides. You grab a knife and fork and bring it to him on the couch. He sends you back into the kitchen for salt and pepper, which he doesn't use because you actually seasoned it well enough while cooking it. You go back into the kitchen and clean up.

Thad wolfs down half of it before he notices you slouching in the kitchen doorway, looking at your feet. "You hungry?" he asks, or demands, depending on your point of view.

"Yeah," you mumble because even though you ate what you didn't think he'd notice, it wasn't enough.

He hands you his plate and tells you to finish it. You get about a third of what you cooked.

It's close to midnight by then and you are neither dead nor maimed. He tells you to brush your teeth and take a shower.

You're extremely surprised and somewhat alarmed when he joins you in the shower. You're afraid to look at him, and can't anyway because he starts washing your unkempt brown hair that almost reaches your shoulders.

Thad's really into washing your greasy mop. He turns you to face him and pushes you back until your lathered head is under the shower stream.

You feel his half-hard cock against your thigh. This doesn't freak you out as much as that you're getting hard, too. And get really hard when he grabs your scrawny dick and pulls your scrawny body into his arms and starts rubbing his cock against you.

"You like guys?" he asks, his face buried in your neck. It might as well have been a statement because all you can do by then is moan in something resembling assent.

You cling to him to stay upright when he slides a soapy finger in your ass. And then two, not very gently, but you like it rough. He has you pressed against the very clean tiles you scrubbed earlier, you can hear them squeak against your bony shoulders as he humps you hard into them while ramming his fingers in your ass. You come first because you have no self-control whatsoever, but he comes a few seconds later. Maybe he forgets who you are, but he lays a long, mouth-grinding, tongue-thrusting kiss on you before he tells you to go get in the bed. You do this because you're a little cock-slut and it never occurs to you to escape while he's finishing his shower.

You are sitting naked on the edge of the still-made bed when he comes in, also naked. He tosses the towel on the end of the bed, tilts your chin up and eases the head of his penis into your mouth. While he runs his fingers through your damp hair, you suck him, but not very well.

"Have you done this before?" he asks, pulling your mouth off his cock.

"Once or twice," you say, even though the figure is more like four or five times, but that would let him know how completely hopeless you are at cocksucking. You are trying not to stare at him. He's very lean, but has muscles, scars, and his face, framed by lank black hair, is unreadable in the dim bedside lamplight. You thought he was bigger under his leather jacket and jeans, but he's still pretty scary the way he is. You are also unable to hide that you are turned on by him.

"You need more practice," he says, pulling the covers under you back and shoving you into the bed.

He lies on his back and tells you to get with it. You're not a total idiot, so you get between his legs and start sucking his cock again. You're careful with your teeth and use your lips and tongue on it. He's not choking you with his cock or making you lick whipped cream off it or shoving a butt plug in you or hitting you. He's just lying there, stroking your hair while you do your best to suck him off. You begin to experiment with pulsing your tongue on the underside and you suck, moving your mouth up and down as much as you can. You arch up a little so your weight is on your knees and your hands are free to play with his balls and stroke the base of his cock. He seems to like this, at least it sounds that way. He stops you and tells you to hand him the towel. He jacks himself off into the towel. You don't tell him he could have come in your mouth, you just sit there until he tells you to get him a beer.

When you get back with the beer, you stand hesitantly by the bed until he tells you to lie down. He hands you the beer and tells you to rinse your mouth out. You hate warm beer, but you do as you're told. He gives you another one of those enamel-cracking kisses and plays with your dick until it's hard and leaking. He grunts–this might be a laugh, you don't ask–and rubs the pre-come around the head, giving it one last hard tug. He sticks his fingers in your mouth, exploring your back molars, while you suck your own juice off his fingers. He's getting hard again. He pinches your nipples while he rubs his cock on the soft flesh between your hip and thigh. He seems to be thinking about something. Then he reaches across you for the lube.

You know you were thinking about this, you little catamite. You spread your legs really wide when he unscrews the cap. You're almost graceful when he rolls you on top of him and tells you to get on all fours. You do, and he pulls you by your dick so your chest is level with his mouth and he doesn't have to reach so far to slide his lube-slick fingers in your already over-stimulated ass. With your head nearly touching the wall, you nearly lose it when he starts sucking and biting your nipples while he stretches you. You voluntarily bang your head into the wall when he hits your prostate. He might have laughed again, but you're too far gone to care. He spends a lot of time massaging your sweet spot while you lose your tiny fucking mind.

"Don't come," he orders as he rams another finger in.

You're panting and whimpering above him. You've never enjoyed this this much. You push back against his hand, urging him deeper, your dick leaking pre-come on his belly. He withdraws his fingers. You make guttural squeaking noises of frustration. He shoves you onto your back and grabs a condom. While you watch in a lust-crazed haze as he rips it open with his teeth, rolls it carefully down his very hard, very big erection, and quickly lubes it. Good thing you're a bendy little piece of ass, because he nearly folds you in half to stick his cockhead in. He pauses, and this surprises you. You have no leverage with him pushing your thighs against your chest, but you manage to pulse up against him. His eyes fall half closed and he watches you from under hooded lids as he slides all the way in. He lets your legs down enough so you can move under him more.

By now you are completely incoherent and he's fucking you slowly. Forgetting your place, you reach for your own dick and he slaps your hand away.

"You better come from just this," he growls, fucking you harder for your presumptuous behavior.

You, at this point, don't care if he kills you as long as you can come first. But you want to make sure you come first, so you start raising your bony hips to meet his downward thrusts. He likes this, you can tell, but you don't really care. You like this because you can rub your frenzied cock against him. Every time he slams into you, you're a little closer to blowing your wad.

He comes first, this is the story of your life, you fucking loser. But while he's moaning into your neck, he slides his hand between you two and jerks your cock twice against his sweaty abs until you come obediently in his hand. You come so hard, you arch up and lift both of you off the bed, stifling a scream against his shoulder. He wraps his arms around you and murmurs something you don't understand in your ear until you stop shaking.

He rolls off and tells you to get rid of the condom. You're dazed and not quick enough, so he does it himself. You're still lying there, flushed, your scrawny chest heaving, your nondescript brown hair fanned out on the pillow when he comes back. Setting a new beer on the nightstand, he looks down at you, picks up the towel at the end of the bed, uses it on himself and then tosses it to you. He gets in the bed and sticks his arm out. Even you know enough to curl into it. You feel sleepy, but you can tell he's wide awake.

"Hey...what did you say before?" you ask, timidly, even though it took all your bravery to say anything.

"I told you to get rid of the condom," he says, playing with your hair.

"Before that...Spokane? Did you say Spokane? I've never been there," you murmur.

"Feh, I didn't say Spokane, I said spokadna," he says. "It means relax."

"Oh, I never heard it before," you say, feeling stupid.

"It's Polish. You speak Polish?" he asks, and of course you say, "No," because a pathetic punk like you can barely speak English.

You start to doze, but he wants company. He asks you how the coke dealer got his hooks in you. You tell him your entire life story, how your parents divorced and remarried people even worse than they were, how your big sister took care of you and is the only one in the family that still likes you, how you dropped out of high school because it was a stupid and painful place, and you were no good at sports, math or girls. How you then drifted from town to town to city and finally ended up here. You tell him that you like coke too much, but it makes you happy. You tell him you hate this town, all you get are bad deals and cheated in this town. Everyone is against you. You don't whine or cry like you usually do when you tell this story, you're too relaxed to do that, you just tell it. He doesn't seem to be listening, but he doesn't tell you to shut up. You fall asleep mid-sentence.

When you wake up in the morning, Thad has his arm thrown over you. Your ass hurts a little, but you can't help letting a stupid smile crawl over your punk mug thinking about the night before. "What if he likes me?" you wonder insipidly. "What if I could stay with him?"

Dream on, gunsel. You know you mean nothing more to him than a fast easy fuck to kill time before he collects for the coke dealers and kicks you to the curb. Or rather, kicks you into the gutter, where you belong with the rest of the tra–

"You're too hard on me," you say, sitting up with a stupid pout. "I'm not trash."

"What?" Thad squints and blinks at you.

"Um, I said I think the Post Office is open now," you lie like a cheap rug.

"Yeah...Let's do it after lunch," he says, snuggling you back under the covers.

Don't get your hopes up, punk. Thad G is a bad bad guy. He'll keep you around to blow him, then he'll make you service his friends, then he'll start pimping you out, and eventually, when your ass is shot and you're a walking colony of STDs, he'll put a bullet in your brain and leave your diseased carcass in some dark alley for the rats to nibble on before the cops find it. Scum like you and Thad G don't live happily every after. Your kind have grim and stupid deaths preceded by grim and stupid lives that dirty everything you touch and render null any meaning, any hope, any future, any–

Hey, punk! Are you listening to any of this?

You're not listening because you're making happy slutty squealy noises under the covers with Thad.

A year later you're still with him, but in another town and a nicer apartment. After you dragged yourselves out of bed and showered, which took a while, you fried bacon, grilled kielbasa, and made toads-in-a-hole for breakfast. Thad rolled his eyes at these, but ate a lot of them. Then you went to the Post Office. Your sister, whom you don't deserve, did indeed come through for you and you accompanied Thad to Warp Speed Check Cashing. You got $240 back on her $300 check. You handed him the money and started to walk away.

Thad asked you where your stuff was at. You directed him to the place you were staying, where they were holding your stuff ransom for the money they said you owed them. The door was locked, so Thad kicked it in and pistol-whipped the pit bull when it charged. You found your backpack and Thad picked up a large stack of cash next to a larger pile of weed on the kitchen counter. He told you to come on, he drove you both out of town that day and you never went back. When you stopped for food, he made you write your sister a thank you note on a napkin and you mailed it from the next gas station that would sell you an envelope and stamp. They gave you the envelope, but they made you buy the stamp.

Where you live now, no one knows you from before, but lots of people know Thad. They call him Tadeusz, which you can't pronounce, and they talk to him in a language you can't understand. He doesn't translate, except when it's something you need to know, like when he introduced you to his grandmother. You wait tables, serve drinks and sometimes cook in the restaurant Thad's friend owns. You find out later that

Thad's friend is his cousin. You work a lot. They pay you overtime when you work overtime. You give Thad all your wages, but he lets you keep your tips. You leave the bills and change in a mason jar on the kitchen counter, but he never takes any of it. When your tips are high, Thad starts hanging out at the restaurant to find out who the big tipper is. In a year, he's only had to scare off one guy, who was a pest and an idiot anyway. You make good tips because you're good at being a waiter. This makes you feel better about yourself. You start taking more care of your body. You get your hair cut more than often, stand up straighter, and don't eat junk food or do drugs.

You're not sure what Thad does when he's not around. One time you thought you saw him driving a truck. Another time you thought you saw him throwing a biker out of a biker bar called The Swarm. You don't ask him about these things and he doesn't talk about them. He doesn't talk much, but neither do you.

When he's in the apartment with you he watches TV, eats your cooking and fucks you senseless. You begin to understand what the words "making love" mean. You've heard those words on TV a lot, but when you spend afternoons in bed with Thad and you both come five or six times, your tiny mind begins to suspect there's more going on here than just wham-grr-thank-you-sir ass-fucking.

You're happy and it kind of scares you. Thad might be happy; it's hard for you to tell. The first time he laughed out loud, you nearly jumped out of your skin, which made him laugh even harder. When you come back to the apartment after he does, he doesn't smile or speak, but he does stare at you a little longer than he really needs to to recognize you. When your sister came to visit, he wasn't around much, but he did say "hello" and "good-bye" to her. When your mother got sick and your sister called to tell you she probably wouldn't live, Thad answered the phone and took a message. Then he tossed some of your stuff in a garbage bag, went to the restaurant, and, after talking to his cousin, drove you to the bus station and put you on a Greyhound to your sister's place. When you called to tell him your mom had been glad to see you and then died the next morning, he listens to you crying because you can't help it, and then asks you when you're coming home. You're so floored by the word "home," your saintly sister has to get on the phone and tell him, you'll be home after the funeral, which is in a few days. She tells you you have a nice boyfriend and your brain simply cannot process the dual ideas of "home" and "boyfriend" at that moment. Thad meets you at the bus station and drives you back to the place where you live with him. You rethink this on the way there, you think: "My boyfriend is taking me to our home. My boyfriend is driving us home." You chant this in your pea-brain all the way there because it makes you happy. When you get home, you and Thad make love until dawn. You don't know what love is, but you think it must be very much like this because you're so happy.

Not that you deserve to be happy, you worthless little twerp. If there were any justice in the world–

"See? You were wrong about me and him," you say, softly so as not to wake Thad sleeping next to you. "He never did any of the stuff you predicted and I'm still alive."

Fine. Fuck off and live happily ever after, not that either of you deserve it.

But who ever gets what they deserve in this life? And who fucking cares?

The End

Permissions

Many thanks to Jane S, Molly Kiely, Kris A, Lynn L, and Xtian for their stellar editorial support.

Many thanks to Robin Austin for the fabulous cover design.

Please visit our website for more information on this title.

The Wapshott Press
www.WapshottPress.com

www.ingramcontent.com/pod-product-compliance
Lightning Source LLC
Chambersburg PA
CBHW030011290326
41934CB00005B/300